CRISIS: THE NEW BLACK
A CODE TO LIVE BY

A personal-development book by Georgina Popescu

GEORGINA POPESCU

CRISIS: THE NEW BLACK
A CODE TO LIVE BY

A personal-development book

CORESI
PUBLISHING HOUSE

WWW.CORESI.NET

Cover design: Leo Orman
Cover illustration: Georgina Popescu

© 2017 CORESI Publishing House SRL, WWW.CORESI.NET.
All rights reserved.

ISBN-13: 978-1981924226 (CreateSpace)
ISBN-10: 1981924221

The Kindle edition of this book [ISBN 978-606-996-132-2] can be accessed
here: http://amzn.to/2hbiLDs

For more information regarding this book, please write to coresi@coresi.net.

www.coresi.net
www.LibrariaCoresi.ro
www.librarie.website

Motto:
The trouble with our times is that the future is not what it used to be.

Paul Valéry

To Hubert,

Who made this book possible, by accompanying my steps into a new world.

FOREWORD

This book is about life.

Some call it "crisis".

Don't let those fool you.

If you know how to live yours, wisely and enthusiastically, there will be no time for their silly games, because...

Those who just wonder will not know...

Those who don't try will never grow...

Those who don't challenge will not win...

Those who don't say will never mean...

Those who don't do will never have...

Those who don't cook will someday starve...

Those who don't pay respect won't last,

Those who don't get it, will not build a past!...

Those who don't give will never get...

Those who don't rise will never set...

Those who don't get love just strive to survive,

Those who don't spread it, never feel alive!...

Those...

Vienna, January 21, 2012

INTRODUCING MYSELF
AND THIS BOOK

I grew up happy, healthy and respected, in a beautiful communist country, which most people judge without knowing much about.

Professionally speaking, I have been a banker for more than 15 years. And more specifically, a distressed loan recovery banker ever since the crisis managed to hit also the Eastern part of Europe, contradicting (!) the optimistic initial forecasts. Despite the turmoil experienced across more than 15 countries at a certain point in my career, I managed to maintain a sense of happiness, state of health (mental one included) and respect across my peers, in a rather challenging profession.

Such graceful survival was possible because of the love, humor and common sense that were floating all around in my family as well as within the larger community of friends and co-workers.

Don't get me wrong...

...Being happy does not mean that I do not cry my eyes out, grief over the tombs of departed loved ones, burst out in anger or fight like a fierce lioness sometimes...

...Being healthy does not mean I do not experience regular diseases and a couple of more complicated conditions from time to time... it just means that I have successfully healed from all that and currently my temporary earthly pain points migrate daily to different parts of my body, fact which my grandmother used to interpret as a state of reasonably good health.

...And being respected... Well, I've had my fair share of curses (even threw some back) and un-invited "compliments" on the street, experienced strikes of envy, rebellion and various forms of being "put down" (or "to my place"), however I do tend to believe that people who act in an offensive way do not disrespect me, but themselves actually... and I have chosen to exchange trust vows only with those who think highly of mankind in general, of themselves and myself in particular. And I have kept my head up high in this process.

My mother was also the teacher, master cook, concierge, farmer, landscaping artist, interior designer, singer & dancer, poet & eloquent orator, doctor (all possible specializations, psychoanalyst included!), philosopher, project manager, Chief Financial and Chief Operating Officer of the family. My father was acting also as Chief Executive and Chief Risk Officer, practical trainer, procurement manager, poet and stand-up comedy actor, travel agent, occasional cook & carpenter, gardener, stamp collector, lottery administrator, playing cards master, DJ & grand cinema administrator, policeman, prosecutor and judge (funny, it did not feel like a conflict of interest back then), boyfriend admission committee chairman.

Both of them have already switched to a Higher Authority supervisory position—my father quite early (as I was still a child), and my mother almost two decades later (while I was still her child).

Why am I telling you all this? Because this book has a story and it is quite a simple one, same as my family life, which is often described in it.

Right in the middle of my happy, healthy and respected simple life, more exactly in the summer of 2011, while my work took me travelling all around ex-communist Europe, I started to write on my friend's blog[1] (Peter Gluck's[2] Ego-Out project) some thoughts about the world crisis.

The first attempt to explain my perception about its origins was called "Roots". While writing, I understood that the complexity of what brought humanity to this point cannot be wrapped up in one night, therefore went to sleep deciding to keep on posting at least until reaching the magic number of 10 roots. And then, I would stop for a while whatever challenging professional endeavor, and collect those thoughts in a book, then throw it in the ocean of universal knowledge...

Over the next months, while elaborating on the initial idea of root causes of the worldwide trouble, I came to the conclusion that what we experience is actually no longer a "crisis", but a gradual and complex shift to a new paradigm, the beginning of a New World Order, as it seemed to me that nothing could stay the same as it was before. The globalization trend that was considered up

---

[1] https://egooutpeters.blogspot.co.at/search/label/Georgina

[2] Romanian researcher, columnist (info.kappa) and blogger (EGO-OUT, hosting the emerging format of this book), author of the Rules of Problem Solving

to 2008–2009 the solution to all economic and social distress of the world proved to turn itself into a modern day Babylon, in which much more than languages have been tangled!

It was therefore difficult to pinpoint just one culprit for our distress, as there were so many of them, conspiring together or individually, on higher or lower level, thus generating together the perfect storm... insisting to find just one common evil root for all this, would lead me to conclude it should be... the whole mankind!

And so, almost one year after starting the Roots series, even though I was still far from reaching the target of ten chapters, I started to write in parallel another, a more optimistic one—the Ways. It came to life as I felt the need to go beyond merely outlining the causes, and explore where we could go from there—by "we" meaning all those people who would neither accept the doomed path not forfeit our life under the gloomy burden of our times.

The Ways gravitate around one main idea—the need for education. A complex approach that would cultivate more than technical, economic, legal, artistic, scientific and other theoretically and practically oriented sciences. The men and women of the future urgently need to find a way to learn about morals, integrity, ancestral & contemporary wisdom—the sooner, the better!

I do believe that education could be a universal panacea for mankind trouble, but getting the right recipe is no easy task! To define and, moreover, to translate into practice such a therapeutically educational model in a profoundly sick (already metastatic!) society may prove to be more complicated than to discover the formula for the philosopher's stone or elixir for perpetual youth. I do not expect any community to reach perfection in the area of education but this should not stop us, mortals, from trying... starting with our inner circle and gradually extending towards close family and friends. If we act consistently, in good faith and given enough time, we may reach a critical mass that would trigger notable effects on a historical scale.

So... 5 years, 10 Roots and 10 Ways after the pilot episode was written in August 2011, it seems to me that we are still exploring the same "crisis"—the new world, shifting its values and adjusting its masks all around us. And so the book came to life in the year of 2016, the first edition being launched in Romanian, as a gift to my ex-communist fellow countrymen. The current English version is actually not a translation of the Romanian one, and neither the other way around—as I find it hard to express the same ideas in different languages, and I prefer to mold each according to the personality of the next potential reader.

There is no formal order in this book, except the grouping of roots vs. ways, and even so they should just complement each other. You can start with any chapter you like and explore from there—wonder and judge any topic for yourself. Just challenge your imagination and discover new things behind the lines, at least for a while after you close the book. What you are about to read is just a collection of thoughts and personal opinions, subjective interpretations of surrounding reality, that may or may not resonate with your own perception. This is actually the beauty of the chosen topics—one will not find here any statistical evidence, expert research and analysis, conspiracy theories or blame games.

No matter if we agree in our interpretation of what's going on in the world, one thing is certain: we cannot afford to remain indifferent any longer!

Georgina Popescu

SUMMARY

The trouble with our times is that the future is not what it used to be.

Paul Valéry

PART I—ROOTS

"It's no measure of health to be well adjusted to a profoundly sick society."

Jiddu Krishnamurti

"A civilized society is one which tolerates eccentricity to the point of doubtful sanity."

Robert Frost

> *"It is not because things are difficult that we do not dare, it is because we do not dare that they are difficult."*
>
> Seneca

> *"If one morning I walked on top of the water across the Potomac River, the headline that afternoon would read: 'President Can't Swim.'"*
>
> Lyndon B. Johnson

PART II—WAYS

> *"What we are is God's gift to us, what we become is our gift to God."*
>
> Eleanor Powell

> *"Always when judging   Who people are,   Remember to footnote   The words 'So far.'"*
>
> Robert Brault

> *"Patience is the companion of wisdom."*
>
> St. Augustin

> *"Never point a finger where you never lent a hand."*
>
> Robert Brault

PART I—Roots

ROOT 1—THE BEGINNING

Motto:
"It's no measure of health to be well adjusted to a profoundly sick society."

Jiddu Krishnamurti

It was the evening of August 15, 2011 when the chain of events happening all over the world made me want to share with my friends some solitary thoughts about deeper roots potentially attributable to the global distress that was spreading around like a bush-fire.

One year after leaving Romania for exploring the larger Europe, I thought back on the initial bias in my mind—the idea that the communist mentality has damaged a lot of good and capable individuals, and made them somehow unfit for the bigger and better world. I left the country with a perception that envy and hatred, favoritism and corruption, as well as misunderstanding of freedom, social irresponsibility and political unawareness were a local plague. I smiled on the future, hoping that it could be eradicated over time, if only capable enthusiastic people would experience a different environment, learn how to make things better and then come back to translate such learning into reality.

I was at the same time rather skeptical, as I understood that individual well-being may very well prevail in the end and thus the numbers of those who would come back would be rather limited. However, this is another story, which I have explored for more than 10 years now, but will be subject to another book.

Now let's go back to August 15, 2011.

It was about one year after head-quartering myself in Vienna—the Austrian capital of music, coffee and perfect public transportation. After taking a professional deep dive into most ex-communist countries, and getting closer contact with international financial markets, one summer evening while watching the evening news, I started to think about the last few years from a slightly different perspective. I began to wonder... what if the financial crisis, the terrorist attacks, the gloomy future and our unresponsiveness to all those challenges have deeper roots than the US sub-prime and the shock-wave it triggered? What if that was not actually a root cause but just an effect of a much older and deeper problem?

One thing became clear to me—the fact that human nature is the only constant variable (if I may say so...) all over the world. No matter how much we dream about a better future, how much we pray that the world would conspire and converge to our dreams, what we need to face, both in the short and the long run, is... reality happening—every day!

Positive thinking that ignores hard evidence to the contrary is one of the most damaging approaches to life. My experience in dealing with distressed companies has taught me that in order to find a way out of any tough situation one must first understand and address its roots. It may very well be also professional bias, but it proved many times around to be the best way to approach—the faster you spot a potentially damaging event, the sooner you solve it, the better the result and the more sustainable the solution!

With such mind-set, let's surf now through some world events happening back then, in no particular order.

Social crisis—extreme right parties were gaining popularity, as individual aggression was escalating. The shooting in Norway (Breivik attack—the 32 years-old guy who killed 77 people, mostly children, in one day and on two different locations), broke the pattern of the "classical" terrorist definition. People were being buried alive by criminal gangs nearby Budapest; it looked like two years after an exceptional Romanian handball player was slaughtered in a nightclub dispute, the police still did not get them off the street... In UK robberies and street fights were escalating, with no particular criminal profile—all ages, colors, religions or education background. The prime minister in charge back then (Tony Blair) invited to London, as consultant for solving the crisis, the famous "zero-tolerance" New York chief of police—Bill Braton. Meanwhile, conflicts in the Middle East were worsening, with humanitarian implications that the world did not grasp thoroughly enough back in 2011.

Sovereign crisis was also spreading throughout the world.

Several European countries were falling under the scrutiny of rating agencies, having difficulties in refinancing debt while trying to get budgetary deficit under control. Initially only the so-called PIIGS seemed to be in trouble, later on the contagion kept on spreading. Discussion about the future of the EURO-zone was dragging for months, Russia and Ukraine were pulling away from each other and China was already over-heating. The US seemed to have stepped out of the woods after the Congress vote on increasing the debt ceiling on August 2nd; but they just took a couple of breaths and then got hit really hard by a sovereign rating downgrade; the stock market plunged.

All in all, that summer a new shock wave seriously hit the financial world, while the previous one was not fully amortized, and everybody was watching out for a potential tsunami-effect. Countless experts were trying to be the first to specifically predict when the world (as we know it) would come to an end...

Just as in 2008, worries were being expressed in the international media, reminding us the lesson of history: after big economic crisis, wars followed. Ever since then, such theory expanded, making everyone wonder whether the current line of events would lead to a devastating World War III or, even worse—that it is already here, disguised under local and regional wars, financial turmoil, internet attacks and AI rising...

I wonder whether is there anyone that would still remember the "feel good" mood, rushing through their veins many years ago, long before any of the "crisis" symptoms had surfaced? It was a period of glorious growth, which most people thought will never end; it seemed only natural that prices could go nowhere else but up, money be always easy to make, and the spending spree would be the only logic purpose of having all that cash! Saving was not "trendy"; old age was something beyond imagination. Everyone was tempted to seize the day, and then seize also the next day, then the day after... Well, and why not seize them all TODAY? (As it was so easy to get a 35 years credit back then, right?).

Well... those who adhered to this line of thinking were either over-optimistic or ignorant or plain crooks (meaning they never intended to pay back what they borrowed). But they were also many! And it was only a matter of time for those countries where spending was chaotic and individuals over-indebted, as the companies they owned and the governments they elected behaved more or less the same. And that was one side of the coin.

But there was also another side of the coin, especially for the European Union members, after the introduction of single currency—the Euro. Everyone got free access to money, on a new market that was treating debtors more or less the same. And this is how it all went wrong—subprime story on several country levels. Previous to that moment, the local currencies and credit spreads reflected their issuing countries' profile. The access of individuals to loans was also restricted to local market availability (in terms of volume, price, and currency). Once the Euro kicked-in, that control was lost.

Globalization effect in the ex-communist countries included big money flooding the "new" markets after the drop of the iron curtain, brought by profit-oriented organizations, with different mentalities and mind-set about spending. Western world saw the opportunities of enlarging the market for their own products and, as the Eastern bloc did not have enough purchasing power to take on the huge quantity of goods, the suppliers also brought along a matching lending offer.

What they faced here was first of all the lack of historical prosperity in those countries—no prior accumulation and no middle-class. Consequently, not too many second-ways out were possible for bad loans. There was also a significant mass of ignorant and crooks on those markets and completely different legal systems, which worked (or not...), as per local standards.

Global lenders aggressive expansion policies and high competition did not help either, as the labor force was not so well prepared. To cut it short, there was either lack of market-oriented professional and managerial capabilities (as most senior professionals were educated in the former communist spirit) or a complete lack of know-how (as the young and junior people were theoretically well trained but practically inexperienced).

Thus a vicious circle was put in motion whenever ignorants and crooks started to look at each other over the counter.

Do not get this wrong—the rule of thumb was of course to a large extent the qualified professional (both on customer and staff level), but I would not explore here the normality, as in such case the system returned expected results. However sometimes other scenarios may have occurred: whenever one ignorant met one crook (or the other way around) small personal profits were gained and hidden within the system; whenever two ignorant met, the balance could go each way; but whenever two crooks met, then huge personal profits could be gained and hidden within the system.

Of course that all the above common sense considerations were pondered by the risk analysis of global investors that came into those countries and translated into higher "risk premiums" than what was practiced on mature markets. Basically, this would be transparent by comparing the prices that companies and individuals need to pay for similar services. However, the analyst could not measure this very meticulously, as they never experienced any cyclicality in those environments.

Consequently, the advanced economies are still gradually paying the bill on those developing markets which they have artificially inflated, to sell out their own products. At the same time, the good-faith borrowers and the competent professionals will have to pay even more "risk premium" in the future—for the ignorant and the crooks unveiled during the financial crisis.

And this is only one tiny little part of the overall global distress story, and only the European flavor. The world is much bigger and the problems much deeper. Since 2011 further aggravating events have happened, starting with a huge migration wave (from the war-zones in the Middle East & Northern Africa to continental Europe), the earth-shaking Brexit that put to shame all the other XX-exit worries (Greece included!), the raise of the nationalist parties and autocratic leaders all over the world, and the US election 2016 Black Swan[3] effect.

Regarding the sovereign crisis and financial distress hovering over Europe, in my opinion the recent years were spent in denying reality while rolling the snowball, by gradually shifting the burden from the private sector to the public contributor, through an invigorating mechanism similar to the US's Quantitative Easing[4]. The non-performing loan tsunami will not be broken by passing the hot potato from one owner to the other, and those troubled economies must first bury the dead horses and fix their losses be-

---

[3] The Black Swan theory (introduced by Nassim Nicholas Taleb in his 2007 book, named after this theory) is constructed around the idea that certain events, unexpected and apparently unforeseeable for the observer, may generate systemic effects with major and abrupt impact; predicting such trigger events is difficult (border to impossible), however afterwards, when analyzed in ret-

fore moving forward, if they really want to come alive out of a very long winter...

To cut it short, as this is not a book on economic theories, I will go back now to the common voice of global experts mentioned before. Some have attributed the escalating social and political unrest to the financial crisis, further linking this to the historical experience of long-term depressions leading to dramatic world wars.

And the question that popped inside my mind was: "what if they got it wrong?" What if the global crisis was not a root cause, but just one of the many effects of a much deeper and older problem?

In order to build on this idea, I needed to dig out the official explanation of the 2008 events and simplify it to an extreme, for the purpose of exemplification. Back then, the main culprit identified was the sub-prime mortgage lending in the US. The effects spread throughout financial world and real economy almost at the same time, like a metastatic cancer in the last stage.

Some analysts are still questioning whether the State intervention in the US (followed by a more hesitant Europe later on) was more likely just a palliative treatment, while the cancer kept on spreading. On the one hand, there was the Quantitative Easing mentioned above, stimulating consumption by means of increasing the mon-

rospective, they are perfectly explainable and can be rationalized in a coherent manner.

[4] Alternatively known as Large Scale Assets Purchases, it is a monetary policy in which a central bank creates new electronic money in order to buy government bonds or other financial assets to stimulate the economy (i.e., to increase private-sector spending and return inflation to its target) / Source: https://en.wikipedia.org/

etary base, on the other hand there was the long-term preservation of a very low reference rate (practically zero), with the intended purpose of encouraging spending and re-launching lending activities.

On the short run, both intervention measures can be effective, however maintaining them over a longer period of time may generate adverse effects. One such consequence may appear upon sudden return to normal self-regulated parameters i.e. after the intervention window has been closed. In case the economy is not healthy enough and the growth cannot absorb and sustain those additional costs, it may fall back to an even steeper crisis (the W-shape type). Another consequence is when, in order to avoid such an effect, the intervention window is either kept open for too long or the closing is pursued gradually over a long period of time—in such cases, the economy may experience a full economic cycle under false premises and may start going down on its own, while the State is left without enough margin for intervention to generate a positive effect any longer. The second approach is being pursued by the US right now (quite late in the process), while Europe has not started to close the window yet.

Coming back to the evening news on August 15, 2011, I was watching experts talking about the world facing a completely new challenge—the sovereign crisis, significantly more complex than the one that hit three years before. Yet I could not see the difference in the pattern behind, just a more politically exposed set of actors: on the one side, good-rating countries using the opportunity of favorable lending prices, triggering over indebtedness and thus spending more that "they" could afford (yes, those political majorities that "we" have chosen). On the other side, "we" (the contributors) would obviously not be able to repay such debt in our lifetime—our children and our children's children would need to keep paying for what "they" spent in the last few years. It could be considered fair enough only if our children could actually benefit from what was built or created with that money—infrastructure, education, research. In such case there would be a reason to contribute their share to the repayment of the money spent. But if money was wasted on social privileges, fueling inefficient state apparatus, and investing into useless things, then our offspring would certainly have a moral issue to pay for that.

And so I came to a personal decision taken that same hot summer evening. I started writing down some ideas about tolerance and the balance we should reach within ourselves as individuals and then disperse in the community around us, in order to keep our constructive good intent and prevent the world from slipping into a dangerous territory. As I was writing, I quickly realized that tolerance was just one of the many things to explore, if I was to really dig down some deeper roots of the crisis.

And so, at the end of that day, I decided to rename the blog posting and called it "Roots"—the first one out of a longer series with this theme.

That evening I went to bed with the feeling that the global mess might very well be a long-term systemic effect of something which started with the best intentions, some 60 years before. Humankind seems to be facing a moral crisis, rooted in the contemporary misunderstanding of basic human rights. My mind strolled back to 1948, when the world was still struggling to define the basis for peace after World War II and the United Nations passed the Human Rights Magna Carta. It was one of the most beautiful efforts to honor and preserve humanity, the triumph of good over evil and modern civilization as we know it would probably never exist without the efforts of our predecessors to promote those rights.

At the same time, the roots of current crisis may very well be traced back to the way our contemporary world understands, interprets and chooses to respect and enforce those rights. More exactly, it has to do with how far the humanity strolled away from their fundamental idea, by gradually separating rights from corresponding obligations. After a few generations, individuals lost the collective memory that encompassed the very reason for writing the Magna Carta and they are now dominated by the self-delusion that life is only about having rights, without offering anything in exchange!

There are many religions, social, political and legal systems in this world; yet, in the name of the basic human rights, there is a huge pressure towards converging the entire world to obey by some common "universal" rules. Without being wrong, it is also not fully right. Over-complicating the human rights principles, expanding them into minimum social and/or economic rights, interpreting and applying them differently in various environments and even worse, misusing their concept on individual or social levels has thrown the global human into a trap similar to the paradox of tolerance.

Tolerance is praised nowadays as the key towards understanding between all people, as the ultimate virtue that must be universally practiced in order to get everything in good order. Of course that "good order" in the view of tolerance is that I would let you do whatever you want even though I disapprove and it is wrong as per my standards. Alternatively, being intolerant means that I try to stop you and inflict my view of right and wrong upon you, which would be breaching your basic human rights. Tolerance does not seem wrong as a basic concept; however it is a fine line between tolerance, acceptance and then practice. And this is where Pandora's Box opens, and you can read more about it in the next chapter.

The technological progress further deepened the rift between people and reality, encouraged the development of parallel universes (virtual but not only), in which everything seemed possible and easy to control. Excessively promoting the idea of positive thinking also generated several side effects such as denying the reality, postponing or even avoiding the solving of real problems. Practical education and hard-work has become redundant and is mostly replaced by theory and programming, while human component has been gradually taken out of regular communication. All in all, we are witnessing the erosion of applied common sense in our day-to-day living.

What else is there to say? As per the interpretation of the Maya calendar, the world has already ended, in 2012... Let's be optimistic once again and assume that a large part of us would still be able to beat the odds.

We are now six years after that evening of August 15, 2011, when everything seemed to converge towards a scary future. Yet we are still standing and, moreover, it looks like humankind has grown closer to understanding the roots of its global distress. And therefore also keener about finding solutions.

It is a more complicated New World Order, with fragmented players and a blurry mix of financial and political power, which turns any thread of social responsibility into thin air. Promises are periodically wrapped in some new colors, but the same smoke screen comes out every now and then, preventing large masses from seeing through the real world.

But people are gradually developing a third eye, to see behind that smoke. My hope is that this book may assist anyone interested in exercising that, for the benefit of living beautifully in the New World—while still alive!

ROOT 2—THE TOLERANCE

Motto:
"A civilized society is one which tolerates eccentricity to the point of doubtful sanity."

Robert Frost

Let's start exploring one of the most controversial concepts in human history, by taking a look at a couple of Wikipedia[5] definitions.

Tolerance is "the practice of permitting a thing of which one disapproves, such as social, ethnic, sexual, or religious practices" or, summarizing from a more detailed DEX[6], the act of toleration involves cumulatively a form of aggression (physical or psychical) together with a form of acceptance without reaction / retribution, basically meaning that the aggressed one consciously chooses not to react, even though he/she has the ability to do so, but is convinced that such inaction would benefit everyone in the long run—on both personal and social level.

----

[5] Source: https://en.wikipedia.org/

[6] Summary and interpretation based on dexonline.ro i.e. Romanian language definitions of tolerance / to tolerate

The paradox of intolerance is described as the fact that a tolerant person might be antagonistic toward intolerance, hence intolerant of it; the tolerant individual would then be, by definition, intolerant of intolerance. It is almost like a circular reference in an Excel file, but it does not come either with the warning "you have just created a circular reference" or with a quick "fixing" solution. We just have to deal with it as it comes.

The paradox of tolerance is a little more complex and I also refer you to Wikipedia for a proper understanding of it and hence use Karl Popper description, from his book "The Open Society and its Enemies" (1945): "Unlimited tolerance must lead to the disappearance of tolerance. If we extend unlimited tolerance even to those who are intolerant, if we are not prepared to defend a tolerant society against the onslaught of the intolerant, then the tolerant will be destroyed, and tolerance with them. (...) We should therefore claim, in the name of tolerance, the right not to tolerate the intolerant."

I remember a Romanian joke about tolerance in a marriage: she tolerated his promiscuous behavior, he tolerated her promiscuous behavior, and therefore they were living together in a tolerance house (Romanian synonym for a red-light house).

Tolerance is praised nowadays as one of the key pre-requisite to globalization, communication and mutual understanding between all people, the ultimate virtue that must be universally practiced in order to get everything in good order. Of course that "good order" in the view of tolerance goes like that: I would let you do whatever you want, even though I disapprove and it is wrong as per my standards. Alternatively, being intolerant means I would try to stop you and inflict my view of right and wrong upon you, which would be breaching one of your basic human rights.

Tolerance is the twin sister of freedom, one of the three fundamental concepts born during the French Revolution (together with equality and brotherhood).

In other words, I am free to do as I please, you MUST accept and let me do it. Or... I am free to do as I please, you ARE NOT FREE to choose if you want to endure this or not. Well, we already have a breach!

Anyway we turn this, in a dual report that assumes "ex ante" that tolerance should be present, we have a breach of this basic human right (freedom to choose, act, react...) by one of the parties. In order not to obtain this, the decision to tolerate something must come willingly, by free choice, from the one who is the subject of respective aggression. And such a choice always depends on a large array of influences, starting with education, going through the characteristics and intensity of the aggressive act, the subjective interpretation of the consequences, the context, environment, external expectation and so many more variables—for each of the parties involved!

On the other hand, being intolerant would mean that the one who is mistreated could prevent the other from doing something and strive to inoculate instead his/her own vision of right and wrong, good or evil, normal or abnormal, proper or improper. This might also represent a breach of several human rights, the most important being again the freedom of thought, or choice, or action—that should be aligned to one's beliefs.

Finally, there would be a large degree of interpretation whether in a specific situation we deal with breach of human rights or need for tolerance at all—and that is whenever the involved parties start to exchange views and have a reasonable argument, at the end of which one may embrace the other one's opinion and therefore the situation could end up in a consensual alignment.

As a conclusion, the result would always depend on the balance of power, negotiating skills and specific context of any encounter.

Tolerance is not bad at all as a base rule in our contemporary society, quite the contrary—it allows diversity of opinions and constructive dialogue and it has a preventive role in case of conflicts that would otherwise uselessly escalate. Moreover, from a historical perspective, it is safe to say that after thousands of years of abominable persecution and extreme intolerance, humankind has progressed towards a better life especially thanks to its predisposition towards increased tolerance.

But then... let us go one step further. Even though it does not seem wrong as a basic concept, there is a fine line between tolerance, acceptance and practice. This is where a Pandora's Box opens, as history has proven that things which are initially forbidden are practiced in secrecy, and bashfully tolerated, then brought to public knowledge more and more, until they are gradually accepted and finally turned into normal habits for increasingly larger part of the population.

And this is why I came to see the excessive praise of tolerance and political correctness as one of the main roots of our current crisis. Even though the Human Right's Magna Carta stipulates the necessity of educating our societies towards tolerance and while the benefits of such approach are rather obvious, the direction in which such education may lead us in the future is dangerously difficult to foresee. Sliding towards extremes (tolerance or intolerance) may throw entire nations into any of the above described paradoxes. The balance is hard to set, has both individual and social triggers and consequences, while the history is full of flourishing empires or civilizations that had self-destroyed.

Everybody gets his / her unique perception about good and bad during the years of elementary education, first in the family, and afterwards in school. Later on, one grows further, within the boundaries of personality, circle of friends and experience. The individual tolerance level is finally influenced by many factors—from character to context, circle of comfort and instinct of survival (sometimes it is purely dangerous to be intolerant), perception about own dignity and basic rights, protection and love (we can be very tolerant when it comes to ourselves but extremely intolerant when it comes to threats to our children or loved ones).

Unfortunately, we have become immune to many bad things that happen around us, often choosing to create and protect our own microenvironment, while assuming that as long as we do not hurt or bother other people, they would also not interfere with us.

We tolerate bad service and rude behavior, inefficient management and corrupt politicians, expensive but low-quality service. Even more, it seems to me that we tend to endure more frequently exactly those things that we can actually change (maybe not easily but still... within our power!); but we are too laidback or afraid or plainly not motivated enough to act. We pursue so often our personal gain that we have almost forgot to do things just for the simple reason of being right and proper. On the other hand, we are quick and loud in publicly showing our disappointment and "intolerance" either towards petty little things that do not matter or towards exactly the opposite—major global problems, which we know will not be changed simply by our manifest of intolerance.

In case you still wonder what does this have to do with the global crisis, my answer would be: potentially everything! One of the root causes of current turmoil lies in the clash of civilizations. We all live in a kind-of-a-Babylon-City only that this time the stage is the entire world and there are almost 7 billion actors. We all preach the path of tolerance, but the huge diversity does not allow us to make the further natural step towards acceptance or the bigger step towards uniform practice. In exchange, we inflict every day on each other all those things that we believe in, just assuming that the other would tolerate this, and without understanding that at a certain point in time, their comfort line is likely to be crossed. And I am not referring now only to big issues such as race & color, religion & belief, culture & history, tradition & habit, value & morale, social & political systems etc. I am talking about much more simple things from our day to day life.

I remember one University professor asking us why we think there was no movie about the life of a normal teacher—someone that studies, gets married, has children and teaches other people until retirement and then goes to a village and enjoys the silence and flowers and family for the rest of his happy life. Nobody reacted, so he gave also the answer: because such a normal life pattern would be boring for anyone to watch. On the other hand, he invited us to take a 2-hour action-movie and try to live at that pace every day for at least one year. He would bet that nobody would make it out of this experiment alive, and if they do, would not want to watch another action movie ever again… people would just dream about retiring in a village, and forget about business schemes, secret lives, complicated intrigues and painfully twisted love stories.

Perhaps he was right or maybe the truth lies somewhere in the middle—one month of adventurous vacation alternating with one year of normal life would probably be just fine for most people.

Coming back to the topic, diving into diversity as a challenge and using tolerance as a survival tool may be interesting as an occasional case-study, touristic attraction or movie scenario, but not for everyday living over extensive periods of time. At a certain point people need to withdraw in their circle of comfort and get on with their normal life.

And for this purpose one builds family and friendships, develops long term commitments and abides by a set of self-satisfactory values on an individual level. On a social level, we empower other people to take care of those other things, which are presumed to be "ensured" with our money and votes, as part of our basic human rights.

However... if we do not break our circle of comfort from time to time, to exercise control and corrective measures on the people we mandate to rule our society, in the long run we will have no guarantee that they actually fulfill their tasks. Because human nature will make them take shortcuts and find easy ways out of any trouble they had created. Sometimes they may forget the scope for which they were elected, other times they underestimate the level of responsibility or (even in good will!) misunderstand the mandate they were given.

When a child does something wrong (and is caught), he/she is punished by the parents until he/she learns how to behave. When a mature individual does something wrong (and is proven guilty), the punishment should be applied by the justice system designed and maintained by the beneficiary society. When a group does something wrong (which is publicly disclosed), the usual punishment is marginalization or even extinction of that group from the social and political life. But when a society does something wrong... it is very hard to expose and even harder to correct!

In my optimistic view, I choose to believe that no matter how deep the trouble, once it is properly defined and assumed, at least one realistic solution can be identified. Thus, in case of mankind, it has become obvious that there are deep moral roots that led us to the crisis we are facing nowadays. The sooner we understand that the change must start within each one of us, the faster we shall get our heads above the water again. For sure we would not be able to put all the bad things back inside Pandora's Box, as the idea of reversing the globalization trend is not just difficult to implement, but also completely insane even to try. We just need to find a way to adapt and survive under a new paradigm. The good news is that we are an easily adaptable species.

So, just one question left to answer: to what should we adapt?

Each one should look for the answer to that question, so I will share mine with you.

I believe we should start by stopping to believe that there is a perfect country somewhere in the world, inhabited by perfect people, with perfect economy and perfect social and political system. We are all so predictably human and at the same time so unique, that we have to start understanding and admiring diversity of civilizations just as much as we appreciate the same in individuals.

After all, societies are living creatures and it should be fascinating to understand their personality and respect their power. In order to facilitate our own individual evolution, we need to learn how to refrain from projecting distorted expectations on those countries where we choose to live. Once we accept the necessity of this basic synergy, we should be only one step away from identifying a dynamic balance between tolerance and intolerance on a social level, which would allow us to become comfortable on an individual level, without sliding into the paradox trap.

Finally, we should not forget that in the absence of such individual comfort, public hypocrisy may prove even worse than manifested intolerance, as it encourages accumulation of socially repressed discontent, which is in itself a time bomb.

ROOT 3—THE PROVIDER

Motto:
"'Ohana' means family—no one gets left behind, and no
one is ever forgotten."
Chris Sanders and Dean DeBlois, Lilo & Stitch

One of the most visible manifestations of the global crisis, briefly mentioned in the first chapter, is the sovereign debt crisis, meaning an increasing number of countries unveiling their inability to support future spending, under conditions of high accumulated indebtedness.

Sovereign debt crisis is different from actual default but, whenever not recognized and addressed early in the process, it can very well end up in default. Basically, a State, without actually seizing the repayment of its due debt, is confronted with a significant increase in debt service and/or lending costs, to the point of unsustainability. The main trigger is when the creditors, noticing the escalation of overall indebtedness and misalignment with future revenue sources, estimate a higher probability of default and thus ask for higher interest when negotiating renewal, refinancing and/or increase of the loans.

The classic example that comes to mind in the European area is, of course, Greece. There are several others, respectively the so-called PIIGS[7], but not only. There is obvious financial distress in the peripheral economies of the European Union, especially after the creation of the Euro zone. Moreover, everybody should be aware that virtually no country is spared from potential debt crisis in the future, as the social protection systems that have been created in the modern years are not sustainable on the long term.

I believe it is not reasonable to link sovereign debt crisis to the failure of a certain state model—be it liberal (capitalist and/or market-driven) or controlled (either communist or religious-driven); it is also not necessarily connected only to local culture, working environment and efficiency, saving and spending habits.

Let's look into the internal matters of the State with a 6-years-old view of things, in order to facilitate a simple understanding.

Just like a regular family, the State is confronted every month with a need to balance its spending according to the revenues. Of course that the spending structure is very complex, therefore I shall group them (for the sake of simplification) in three big categories—social protection, administrative and investment. In the family parallel, this would mean providing for of the old, the young and the disabled, managing the house & related administrative tasks, and investment. In order to cover all necessary expenditure, the State, just as a regular family, may need to compensate for temporary deficit by contracting loans. A sovereign debt crisis appears whenever the financial burden assumed in order to close the deficit becomes overwhelming.

---

[7] Portugal, Italy, Ireland, Greece, Spain

Let's look now for potential causes in each of those three categories.

I will start with the social protection systems, which raise concern both regarding the long term sustainability and the difficulty of short term adjustment. Some critical analysts have compared them to pyramidal schemes (a kind of Ponzi but without the fraud element). Specifically, in order for the beneficiaries to receive their allocated amounts, the contributors must be numerous enough and their contributions sufficiently big to sustain the construction. While in a pyramidal game there is a general rule of "first-in, first-out" (provided you go out in time!), in the social protection system the rules are more complex and priority is not always transparent. Moreover, there is a reasonable predictability only regarding the pension needs, while the other parameters (unemployment, child support, health etc.) are more volatile in the short run. As a rule of thumb, the longer the downside curve in an economic cycle, the higher the pressure on the social assistance mechanism.

Inside the European Union, a stress factor of rather recent date is the freedom of movement inside EU borders. The labor force is migrating from poorer to richer countries, usually during periods of economic growth (when there is high demand for supplementing local work force), with an apparent positive impact on the latest, at least on the short term. To be more specific, the individuals that choose to relocate usually belong to the hard-working contributor segment (young and middle aged), leaving the "exporting" countries with a double deficit—on the labor market and on the tax balance. When the economic cycle turns negative, the "importing" countries may experience an adverse effect, as the immigrants could become beneficiaries of the social assistance mechanism. Finally, on the long term the net effect on the receiving country may also prove to be negative, considering the aging forecast for the European population.

The second major category of expense is represented by the administrative ones—fueling the State apparatus. It is a highly heterogeneous class, covering a large variety of roles and depending on the degree of State intervention in the economy. The financing mechanism is rather similar to the one described above, but on a much larger scale and involving different actors. Just for simplification, I will consider as main revenue source all the taxes collected from the population and active economic entities.

A major factor affecting the tax base is the capital availability on the market, respectively the vulnerability of the private sector in front of local and external influences (direct investment in real economy). The migration of the labor force inside EU borders represents a stress factor also in this case, impacting both State and private sector, however with a higher amplitude on the latest, as it is also the most competitive.

Last but not least, the third category of State expenses is represented by investment, a complex area that I will not explore much, but will stop only on what is relevant for the current topic. Investments need great efforts and present specific cycle that must be followed by the financing structures designed to implement them. Government spending is a major intervention tool in any State policy and it has a huge influence (good or bad...) on the macro economic cycles and long-term prosperity of a nation.

Regarding the probability that investment expenditure would trigger a sovereign debt crisis, it can be illustrated in a simple way. In case short-term lending is used to finance long-term investment it can dramatically accelerate a debt crisis, because the State would need to renew frequently high-value loans and the creditors may spot the weakness and increase interest rates. In case the financing is correctly linked to the investment cycle, on the long term there will be periodical peaks in the debt service, which must be associated with increased revenues in the period; any misalignment of such correlation would then trigger a debt crisis.

Now that we have a fair picture of the simplified structure of a State budget, let's see what happens when it becomes unbalanced. Just as in any normal family, the State would need to adjust.

To keep it simple, there are three alternatives: increase the taxes, cut the expenditure (either in terms of value or in terms of eligibility of the beneficiaries /narrowing the coverage) or contract loans to cover the temporary deficit.

The last option is both useful and usually exercised, under condition that it addresses specific needs, has a temporary nature and is not excessively burdensome in terms of costs, in line with market conditions. In any case, it should be doubled by real efforts to identify and implement feasible mechanisms that would re-balance the budget from a longer term perspective. Because equilibrium between ensuring short-term liquidity and long-term safety net (savings) or at least affordable indebtedness is the key to happiness in any family.

Now let's go back to the main topic of the "roots": the historical evolution of the human rights.

Sometime after the WW2, the basic list was significantly enlarged in many materially relevant areas, one direction being the economic, social and cultural rights[8]. Since then, the world population dramatically increased in numbers, work efficiency rocketed given scientific and industrial progress, life expectation extended significantly. At the same time, health care and education became much more expensive, while local and international migration (to the industrial areas, respectively to the most developed countries) became a global trend.

During election periods, every political party makes popular promises to gain votes, and so the State becomes more generous every 4 or 5 years. Once instated in power, the ruling party faces the crude reality of the budgetary deficit, the disproportion between what is needed and what is actually available. Unfortunately, solutions are mostly applied with short term mind-set, in order to keep the boat floating until the next elections, and then the stakes are raised again, while the snowball keeps on rolling down the hill.

On the one hand, the countries with a historical track record of prosperity, experience of several economic cycles and certain level of political awareness are less exposed to the risk of major unbalance. On the other hand, democracies under construction have neither the maturity nor the resources to implement articulate policies and this is why they are confronted with escalating problems. And finally, the cultural and behavioral patterns of the population are usually mirrored by the local administrative governance models.

The political leaders are basically torn between two categories of expectations from their voters. The first one is encouraging macro-

[8] See http://en.wikipedia.org/wiki/Right_to_social_security

economic growth—target that can be reached by reducing the taxes, simplifying legal and fiscal procedures, developing the infrastructure and stabilizing the local business environment. The second one is providing for the under-dog, ensuring a reasonable social protection for those individuals who cannot support themselves. Addressing the first expectation only provides indirect election capital, as the economic growth depends on many complex factors, difficult to influence and partially unpredictable. Responding to the second one has a direct effect on the target segment of the voters, but also on the budgetary deficit!

Those two intervention tools are also in direct competition with one another—one is reducing the revenues, the other one increasing the expenditure. Given such a double negative impact, theoretically the State could apply them cumulatively only during the economic boom periods, whenever budgetary surplus is expected. Practically this is just another paradox that historically fueled a fierce debate between economists, about the role of the State in an economy... is it better to intervene pro or anti-cyclical?

I feel now the need to stop exploring this economic paradox, as it would exceed the simplification frame I have been constructing. It does not take a genius (either in economics or in mathematics) to conclude that the system is deemed to overheat. Year after year the budgeting process would reveal higher spending needs, while the revenue component would not match its dynamics. For a while, contracting new debt would seem like a cheap and reasonable solution, but in the long-term it always proves to trigger a vicious spiral.

Coming back to the human right discussion, on the one hand we have the beneficiaries of the human right (also called "the under-dog"), those individuals that cannot fully support themselves from own revenues, therefore the State would promise to ensure "an adequate standard of living[9]" (decent housing, health services, daily meal). On the other hand we have the suppliers of the human right, respectively the contributors who share part of their revenues with the previous. The relationship is not direct, as the State assumes the tasks of matching those two parties and administers the social support—for raising kids, for the unemployed, for the retired, for the disabled etc. And every year the budgets have to be drafted and sufficient revenues identified for properly fueling the system.

To this picture, we must add also the resourcefulness of human kind in terms of finding the easiest (or should I say laziest?) way for survival. Remember Darwin? I would say that his theory still applies perfectly to today's life. People migrate from weaker social systems to stronger ones and make use of their best features and this is one of the reasons why the predictability of those systems is further weakened by variables which they could not dimension properly (or even foresee at all!).

In other words, no matter how efficient and stable a system seems to be, under current global conditions it can become vulnerable and unpredictable when it is subject to external pressure that was not present at the time when the initial scheme was designed. Like with any given structure, there is a maximum tolerance point beyond which unbalance starts to manifest.

As a consequence of the inherent need to re-equilibrate their budgets, the most developed countries have quite high (and con-

8 See http://en.wikipedia.org/wiki/Right_to_social_security

tinuously growing) tax burdens, while the less developed ones have (still) relatively lower taxes, but high (and continuously growing!) debt.

And here comes the vicious spiral.

The first question would be: who is granting those loans?

Ten years ago a reasonably fair answer would have been: the financial markets. The private capital was keen to grant sovereign loans, especially inside the Euro zone, considered a safe heaven.

Starting with 2010, the world has changed. The sovereign debt burden of the troubled countries has been gradually transferred from private banks to international financial institutions and that means that if further increase in debt proves necessary, the financing will come from the same source.

It also means that when (not "if", but "when") something will go wrong with the reimbursement, the loss will translate into further increase of tax burdens in those creditor countries.

Is this sustainable? Is it fair and reasonable? Was this the purpose of extending the human rights?

I must admit that I do not know the answer to any of those questions.

So I will rephrase: what can we do? Is there still a window of opportunity for real change?

Do not get me wrong: I fully understand the noble purpose of the social systems, however let's make a reasoning exercise: how did people survive before those systems were created? How do people subsist today in those countries that do not have the same understanding and rules about human rights as those existing in the developed countries?

My answer to that question would be quite simple: family and community. The family is the provider for its children, unemployed, disabled and old (retired) members. The family decides who is offered the opportunity to get proper education and later provide a higher income; who will stay home and provide hard labor and basic education for the children. The family will not abandon its disabled and old people, as it also has a social standing to maintain; while the community would support the established, honest and trustworthy families through their time of hardship.

This is how the society used to work. The family balanced the budget and protected its microclimate in order to provide for its members. One step higher, the community did that when the family was in crisis. The State also provided, but for those categories of people who "advanced" important service in return (military, government, legislative, regulatory etc.), more precisely there were pensions however not for everybody. In case you provided a service for the State, then the State provided protection for you in return. No service, no return. You provided only for your family, and then the family was the one providing for you in your older age.

You may challenge this logic by saying it is outdated and futile. I wonder if one could be able to grasp how genuine such a lifestyle still is, in many regions dominated by starvation, prejudice and discrimination—of any kind!

Of course we should not go back in time—once we have walked on the path of illuminated civilization and have reached a certain living standard, giving up what we have conquered is beyond imagination! But we could actually take a big step ahead, towards redefining the central role of the family in the healthy life of a community. How about not expecting all our problems to be solved by the State and remember instead that all great changes come from within?

Nowadays people are raised to be independent and individualist. Family is gradually losing its central place in the economy of human life cycle, partially because now there is a bigger Provider. The evolution of human rights encouraged that very much. My host on the Ego Out blog where this series was born (Peter Glück) says that the most present religion in our lives today is the one he labels as "Moneyteism". I fully agree with him.

The dominant idea in our youngsters' mind is that family commitment is an old-fashioned concept. They live in the moment, love in successive intense episodes, and believe they will not need anyone when they become old and sick. Some even cannot imagine themselves being old and sick, probably because their old and sick part of the family is not there anymore. They cannot learn from the elder's wisdom because they do not spend time together. The little children also get on their nerves or in the best case scenario just bore them to death.

I like very much how this quote summarizes the problem: "the lack of emotional security of our American young people is due, I believe, to their isolation from the larger family unit. No two people—no mere father and mother—as I have often said, are enough to provide emotional security for a child. He needs to feel himself one in a world of kinfolk, persons of variety in age and temperament, and yet allied to himself by an indissoluble bond which he cannot break if he could, for nature has welded him into it before he was born."—Pearl S. Buck[10].

Our children believe already that money can buy anything. Yes, there are many things that can be bought with money, but at the same time so many that cannot! Let's take the classic example of a nasty cold—get a handful of medicine or a pre-packed soup, make some tea and drink it, then get into your bed and suffer for some days. Of course the whole package tastes differently if the soup is made with love and actual boiled meat, if the tea is stirred by someone who is concerned and so on. Being sick while alone may not be the best combination, but after getting better one gets back in the saddle and goes after even more money. The vicious cycle is resumed.

In the end, the only question people should ask themselves is who should be their Provider for old age. If they choose the State for that, they should understand that it is a Moneyteism choice—the State does not stir the tea or boil the chicken, does not hug you and does not tell you that you are FAMILY no matter how old, sick or grumpy!

One more thing: I focused mainly on the money in this chapter; however the same idea applies evenly to education. We rely too much on the State for exclusively providing education to our children, instead of understanding how much we need to contribute to this ourselves. We continuously promote the need to have more women in business and politics, sometime publicly pointing accusatory fingers towards the world for not having enough career women. Still, whenever it is a matter of own free will, we should

---

[10] American writer and novelist, also known by her Chinese name Sai Zhenzhu (1892-1973)

not talk about discrimination or challenge their choice. I admire very much those women who recognize the need for living the motherhood to the fullest and exercising a special role in developing strong families and providing solid education to their children. We should encourage that instead of interfering with it, and focus on channeling the feminine talent towards socially relevant jobs and flexible schedules.

Finally, as I am used to exploring moderate ways, in the end of this chapter I would just conclude that we could altruistically re-model an excessively egocentric way of life, and consequently re-shape the concept behind our social support system. I do not say that we need to shut it down completely, but just resize and redefine its purpose, so that it becomes sustainable in the long run.

Let's look at this crisis just like the Japanese do: name it opportunity and change our ways. It may be too late for preserving a way of living, but it is surely not too late for re-shaping our living, in a different way. And as such, it might be also time to differentiate between our need for the Primary Provider (which should be our family) and the Provider of Last Resort (which could be the State).

ROOT 4—THE PRETENDER

Motto:
"Many of us believe that wrongs aren't wrong if done by nice people like ourselves"

Author Unknown, Source:
http://www.quotegarden.org/

Starting with this chapter I will gradually enlarge the scope, going from the human rights frame to something much more wide spread in the world since the beginning of time—the Human Nature, actually the oldest and most resilient root cause of any crisis.

And I will start this shift with a simple question: WHO created the mess we are in?

Of course, for most humans, the immediate answer would be: Well, THEY did! Followed by a thorough conspiracy-theory involving politicians, business and financial community, those "wise" guys (& girls—to be politically correct!).

In this case I am afraid I would need to insist in my exploration and ask a second question: then WHO are THEY?

Aren't THEY actually our close or distant families, our neighbors or class mates, our boyfriends and girlfriends, our competitors in a football game in school, our rivals or our enemies? Didn't they come from within our communities? Didn't they used to be a part of our live? Aren't they actually us, just making different choices under specific circumstances?

At a certain point in their lives, they have chosen to make compromises, grab opportunities, or just work harder and longer to get where they are now. I am convinced that their close friends and families still love them and are proud of everything they have accomplished. For each of them there is someone out there who is still wiping their tears, holding their hands and hugging them through difficult times, someone who knows very well their weaknesses and deepest fears.

Our world has various layers—individual, social, economic, politic, religious, military, and so on. For each of those, mankind has created applicable rules—either official or purely informal and traditional (law and regulation, allowed and forbidden, custom and tradition etc.). We have also created controls and punishments, and then defined the roles and actors accordingly. And in this process a lot of honest and decent people were involved, but also some opportunists and ill-intended ones.

Let's go one step forward: it is well known that there are some basic principles for success in an organization. One of those is to know the informal structures, at least as well as the formal ones. Why? Because there is almost impossible to perfectly overlap those two. There will always be long-term employees that have certain recognition even if not promoted, while there will always be also people that are promoted or directly employed as managers that do not immediately (or sometimes never) gain the recognition that should come with respective position. For any new-comer in an organization the number one rule is to understand the balance of power and choose a path to acceptance that would align with his/her morale, professional capacity and future plans. I will not go into many details, as there is a separate chapter about the manager, but will put aside for now a simple conclusion: there are always at least two distinctive layers in any reality—the formal and the informal; and this applies to almost everything—structures, rules, controls and so on.

Practically, the challenge is even bigger when we are confronted with more than two realities, which happens all the time and is correlated to the number of involved parties, obeying by the "+1 principle", nicely illustrated by a popular saying about couples after breaking up. It goes like this:

"There are three sides to every divorce story—hers, his and the truth."

In our regular social, economic and political life, when there are many divergent parties involved, the truth multiplies sometimes exponentially. We may think again about the basic human rights or take another common challenge—the international accounting principles! Those are apparently simple rules who aspired to become commonly applicable to a large number of communities. And then came along a myriad of ways of translating, adapting and then using them into day-to-day life, rather differently in each country. And the cherry on the cake is that also the ways to judge whether they are breached or not are seldom comparable.

Just an example of cultural diversity in understanding a certain set of rules: there are countries where whatever is not specifically forbidden, is considered allowed, while there are countries where something not specifically allowed is considered forbidden! You might say it depends on the wording, but it really doesn't entirely—it is significantly influenced by education, tradition, mentality and the capacity of fitting the rules into the customized logic of those who read the same written phrase.

Keeping in mind the different realities as described above, I would still conclude that we have designed our own world on all of those plans, have set their controls and have attributed consistent punishment for not abiding by the onset rules. And finally, we have chosen to believe it should be enough for those to work! How? Well... I could say that each of us would imagine everything actually working as we intended it to work—rather tricky, don't you think?

While learning about fraud many years ago, one specific characteristic got my attention. It was the correlation of triggering factors that must converge in order for someone to decide to act in a fraudulent manner. There should be an expectation of personal gain, which should outweigh the awareness about controls and the magnitude of potential punishment. Various scenarios could fit this—either huge gain, or perception of low controls or negligible punishment.

The same simple definition could be easily extended to other choices we make in life. Fraud is a big messy word, but so are lie or deceit. And even if this may come as a shock to you, I believe that above correlation could be applied to almost every personal action in our life, as well as in our society, on every level of reality. We could link this to statistics and forecasts, advising and consulting, lawyers, and politicians, as well as to ourselves in any day-to-day decisions.

How could this be true? Quite simple: humans tend to weight everything (consciously or not) through the "loss vs. gain" balance, and then act based on the outcome of that comparison. And when I say "act" I do mean act—as an actor. We are all just little (or great) pretenders in our own lives.

When I see my friend in the morning and he/she looks horrible, I would still smile while saying a nice "good morning", instead of putting on a shocked face and spit out something like "OMG, you look so awful today!" The personal gain is that I get a smile back; he/she may even get a good feeling about him/herself. I would most probably not get caught with the lie and even if I get caught, the punishment will not be that hard to live with...

The same logic hits in when people make mistakes. As per applicable rules (formal or informal), they should immediately admit their fault, assume the consequences (punishment) and correct (if possible) the outcome. Some actually do it. However, given the self-protective nature of each human being, usually some other instincts are triggered first, such as conservation and survival. Most people would probably look for various alternatives, based on those three dimensions above. In the day to day life, individuals frequently act in a way that would confer a personal gain, if they believe they can get away with it or the punishment is not that harsh.

I can imagine some readers outraged by such logic, but that could be also because people prefer to believe that they live in a world of white knights and innocent ladies. The truth is they do not—we actually live in a world of pretenders. Some are nice ones, other are pure frauds. And we have also created some dysfunctional mechanisms in our world, as they also work based on pretense. Humanity has established rules that everybody pretends to follow, while there is usually a huge gap between the writer and the reader in any document that we can rely on only one fact: whatever can be interpreted will be, whatever can be misused will be—it is human nature!

In my professional life I have come in contact with a large number of "Independent Business Reviews" (IBRs) and advisory papers, issued by reputable companies. Experience has taught me to focus first on their disclaimers, which may vary from half a page to a number of pages, and is usually the most interesting part of the whole document. The authors include there whatever cannot be mentioned in the conclusions because of "political reasons". The rest of the material is a perfect stage-up for the "right" message, but in the disclaimer they give hints why some assumptions are most probably questionable.

If you know how to read this part, you can determine what questions to ask or whether you should just throw away the entire paper. The funny thing is that most people skip reading it, as they believe it is a "standard" babble that lawyers use to cover their backs if something goes wrong. It is partially true (especially the last part), except that it is not standard at all! It is carefully written for each case, so that an educated reader could take out of it the most important part of what has paid for.

This reminds me of some great jokes in the communist era, connected to the idea of fake reporting and statistics. Everybody pretended that everything was all right, while the production was counted three times and stated as reality...

After the fall of the Iron Curtain, there was a newly discovered freedom of speech and people started to share information. However, the degree of pretense is still huge at all levels—in both private and public companies and organizations, in politics, law enforcement and everywhere else, personal life included. Sometimes I wonder whether those countries are actually hurting themselves by a misconceived sense of freedom for the media. They insist so much on the negative news, because for 50 years they were not allowed to broadcast that, so they miss the good part almost entirely. It seems that, at a certain point, the Eastern bloc became more talkative and transparent than the West and this was not good for further integration and acceptance.

At least on a superficial perception level regarding the progress of democracy in this part of the world, we are self-inflicting damage by exaggerating in exposing only the corrupted side of the society, the tendency towards witch-hunting, indecent exposure and violation of privacy—generally breaching a large number of human rights. It is an approach that destroys credibility and undermines the power balance at any negotiation table around the world, where the developed nations will probably treat us for a long time as second-hand tolerated visitors.

People pretend both as individuals and as social groups (culminating with nations), both on formal and informal levels, trying to protect their personal gain no matter what. Once someone goes down that road, it turns into a vicious spiral, as the more you hide, the more you need to hide.

Some individuals have a sharp sense of rightfulness and moral standard, but that does not mean they do not also look for personal gain in life. It just means that their pursuit is different and usually translates into non-material things. Instead of money and power, good people search recognition and justice. It does not indicate that they pretend less often in pursuit of their purpose but, just like the motto says, people tend to use double standards for judging others. It is virtually impossible to knowingly inflict bad things upon oneself, as it would go against the primordial survival instinct—our very human nature! We may even despise others for using double standards, but at a certain point we will also do the same. It is just a matter of context and time.

Could anyone design a change request for this primordial programming in our instinctual model? Should we even attempt such a change? Nothing drastic, for sure. If everyone would start telling the truth to each other starting tomorrow, I wonder what would happen. I guess we would face an even bigger chaos than now. First of all because we are not used anymore to hear the truth, we need those little white lies to enrich our lives. Second because we have lost somehow the ability to distinguish the truth and it may happen that nobody would believe it anyway. And third, I wonder what truth should we choose to believe—ours, theirs?...

I believe that pure acceptance that we are human and therefore weak should be our first step. Let us remember that, no matter how unique and special are each of us individually, we are still the same in terms of human nature. It would be nice to open up more; even though it would make us vulnerable, it should also allow a sense of natural expression and freedom into our relationships. We could work on self-improvement every day and only then we should explore our fellowmen, striving to understand their moral profile, dreams and motives. Eventually we would gradually gain trust—first in ourselves and then in the person next to us, without ever forgetting that our realities might look different.

Finally, just like in case of fraud prevention, we should start re-designing moral controls and proportionate punishment, and then build on the perception about their effectiveness.

You may call me a dreamer, but I would also love to introduce in every elementary school a new topic—old popular proverbs interpreted for kids. They should start learning from the wisdom of our ancestors about human nature, honor, duty and respect. It could be a way of building up the "prevention" side, educating the ability to recognize crooks, just like our grandparents used to do.

It is a pity that we have either lost that instinctual inheritance, or that we just keep intuitive perception to ourselves, for the sake of an ill-understood political correctness.

ROOT 5—THE DIVERSITY

The year 2011 found me travelling to almost 20 different places in the world. It was amazing to see how much has been built and invented, and how much humankind has progressed towards making life easier, more entertaining, and more comfortable. It was at the same time astonishing to notice how demanding people have become, feeling entitled to receive things they did not work for or struggled to get. There is an impressive willingness to spend money that were not yet earned, given the availability and fashionable nature of generous spending loans.

I am constantly puzzled by one question: why are people no longer satisfied with simple things in life? Why would they not stop to smell the flowers anymore? You know—those nice and symmetrically shaped things admired from the distance... Next thing I start wondering how many times we pass by pure potential for every day happiness, because we are too busy to welcome it into our life, or too self-important to notice.

But then I remember this is not happening everywhere, as there is still a great part of the world where "shopping while already dressed", "eating without being hungry", "exercising without getting anything done", drug consumption and occasional sex are not yet a way of living. There are still places where money earned with great effort would go for modest food and clothing that protects from indecent exposure and keeps warm when the weather gets tough; where the body is fit thanks to every day work; where the clothes and boots are passed from older to younger brother or sister, after being mended from time to time by a loving mother. There are people with honest smile on their face that live a poor life by "civilized" standards and are happy with it.

And there is another (too big!) part of the world where people live a poor and unhappy life, where children might not live long enough to need clothing, where people might not know much about happiness, but neither about unhappiness... The name of their game is survival—no hope, no comparison, no news, and no success stories to show them what happens outside their world.

It is a world full of diversity. Some might label it as inequity; however I would not explore that path today.

During university years and later on in the professional life, I have come across various theories and tests about characteristics of individuals, social systems and organizations. Here are some simple teachings of two such tools: Geert Hofstede's cultural dimensions[11] and Myers Briggs' psychology indicators[12].

Geert Hofstede clustered basic characteristics of a nation initially into 4, and later on 5 dimensions: power distance, individualism (/collectivism), masculine (/feminine), uncertainty avoidance and long-term (/short term) orientation. For organizations, the dimensions are different, i.e. process vs. results-oriented, employee vs. job-oriented, parochial vs. professional, open vs. closed system, loose vs. tight control and pragmatic vs. normative. His work is generally accepted and widely applied, however also criticized because of presumed over-simplification and too general approach of resulting classifications and scorings. However, it is relevant for the purpose of today's exercise i.e. to get a feeling about diversity in terms of traditional cultures, as well as organizational cultures—latest especially booming in our more recent past.

The cultural clash was inevitable, but in the last decade has gained momentum on a double level—mass migration and expansion of global companies. The mobility of nations has been encouraged both by the progress made in transportation and, specifically for the European Union, by free movement inside the extended borders. Escaping conflict zones and relocating entire families to more advanced economies has also become more facile and it is getting harder to distinguish between real distress and piggy-back riding on the human rights sponsored waves of refugees.

At the same time, companies have been promoting global expansion, in search of new output for their over-production. Mergers and acquisitions that involve local players on target markets are usually followed by significant hardship in the subsequent cultural integration process. Only a few understand that this process should

---

[11] https://www.geert-hofstede.com/cultural-dimensions.html

[12] http://www.myersbriggs.org/

be approached with a complex cross-cultural matrix model, addressing both national and organizational characteristics. Most of the times only after collision the owners remember that prevention would have been better than cure—at their own costs!

Regarding a proper integration on an individual level, Myers Briggs indicators may assist in managing that—how a person's thinking and (re)acting pattern can be channeled to the best of their own potential, for the purpose of future development. It is best to have a specialist apply this test, properly calibrated for local culture, as above mentioned differences (Hofstede) also influence the individual perception of the dimensions of this tool.

The result is a combination of four so-called dichotomies for each individual (extraverted / introverted, sensing / intuitive, thinking / feeling, judging / perceiving). The applications are very wide— in a team structure for example, it allows better understanding of the unique abilities of its members, and how can their tasks complement each other to obtain the best results.

The interesting thing about any of the widely available personality tests is that none would return results such as "thief", "serial killer", "fraudster", or "crook". That means that any one of the resulting types of personality could become an "outlaw", depending on a large number of cumulative factors. It is actually a proven thesis that most people would gradually become willing to compromise on basic principles (to the edge of breaching them) when given the opportunity and approached in the way of "small steps". Other aggravating factors are general evolution (or involution) of the principles within the close environment, as well as the perception about opportunity, control and potential gain (already detailed in the previous chapter).

How about breaking down the "outlaw" label into base words such as "out"+"law"—it would mean something that exceeds the boundaries imposed by law.

What law?!

That is the real question!

We have come a long way from the times of Moses, Hammurabi or Ur-Nammu. Even then the difference between basic moral principles, the idea of right and wrong where dramatically different. If you are curious about it, just check out the "10 abominations[13]" (China / Confucianism), by comparison to the "10 commandments[14]" (Christian principles)—they have very few things in common!

Nowadays legal frames have evolved differently in various countries, with two major consequences—the dilution of several moral principles and the conflicts embedded in the international law.

Contemporary rules are so complicated and frequently contradict each other to the point that people may be guilty of crimes without even knowing it (and, as we all know, unawareness is no excuse for breaking the law). Some laws breach the very idea of fairness, common sense and morality—many people know that so well! Not to mention that there are still countries in which law interpretation is purely subject to the good (or bad) will of a dysfunctional system. Finally, one should be aware that there are certain laws promoted by interested influential circles—the privileged few.

Diversity is all around us, with both its good and evil side.

---

[13] https://en.wikipedia.org/wiki/Ten_Abominations

[14] https://en.wikipedia.org/wiki/Ten_Commandments

It is impossible to make everyone think, feel and act in the same way, no matter how much the world would progress industrially and technologically, how well we would learn to communicate, and how tolerant we would pretend to be. We cannot achieve universal understanding of morality and fairness and should be aware that outlaws will always walk amongst us. Even worse, the more the world is striving to converge, the more agile the ill-intended will become, in search of the perfect environment that would keep them "within-law". The adaptability of crooks in this world is remarkable and at a certain point in their evolution, they understood that is would be more productive to officially legalize their own way of doing things.

Having said that, let's be honest and recognize that in a perfect world, both communist and capitalist doctrines could have been successful. The communists would still be happily leaving in their Utopian society, the capitalists would still be profiting in a perfectly functional market economy, with self-adjusting laws of supply and demand. What happened that they all defaulted? Life! A handful of powerful communists have stolen more than the majority could bear, while the crave for freedom of opinion, movement and choice burst out in revolutions; or, as per some theories, the capitalists just needed more playgrounds for their games... and those regimes failed. Another handful, of powerful capitalists, with access to the right tools, started gambling on their free markets, with other people's money. They also decided to "better regulate" those markets, so that no "out-law" principle would get between them and their gains. Classical economic theories are being challenged by new ones, with irrational behavioral patterns and black swans setting the trend.

The good thing is that a lot of progress was achieved on the sideways of this evolutionary process. The non-rich majority (that called themselves at a certain point the "poor and decent 99 %") started living nicer lives, and enjoyed better entertainment than ever. They then orchestrated a couple of decently colored revolutions, a round of emancipation, while entrusting the "rich and rotten 1%" with increased power. Finally they loosened control over the outcome.

So, who is to blame? The bear for eating the honey or the bee for keeping the window opened?

This question may have already lost its relevance, given the severity of current distress.

Let's take another one: what's next?

Personally, I would cast a long-term optimistic outlook on humanity.

Why?

First line of reasoning:

"Everything will be okay in the end. If it's not okay, it's not the end!" Author Unknown[15]

Second line of reasoning: it seems like we are approaching the bottom and...

"History teaches us that men and nations behave wisely once they have exhausted all other alternatives." Abba Eban[16]

We have the strength to evolve, an immense adaptability potential and... strong grandparents! Science revealed that genetic inheritance usually skips one generation, so kids seldom get along with

[15] Source http://www.quotegarden.com/index.html
[16] Israeli diplomat and politician (1915–2002)

their parents, but almost always get along with their grandparents (in my opinion, "spoiling" also has to do with it, but anyway...).

Therefore I will close this chapter with my grandfather's wisdom. He used to say "I wish to reach that degree of poverty that would allow me to provide just enough for my family".[17]

And so he did!

---

[17] In Romanian, grandfather's saying would translate: 'Să fiu sărac, să am ce-mi trebuie!'

ROOT 6—THE CONTROLLER

This chapter is about another root cause of the current global distress—namely the Controller.

A generic description of the four basic pillars which I believe are common to any controlling system can be summarized like this: 1/ "the object" (that can be also a "subject"), 2/ "the current status", 3/ "the desired status" and 4/ "the (corrective) action". Another very important aspect is 5/ "the time constraint"—meaning the maximum allowed period of time for alignment to the desired status.

One of the simplest controlling processes that come to my mind from childhood period is my mother's hand-washing check point. I can still here her voice: "Have you washed your hands? No?

---

[18] American contemporary writer—http://rbrault.blogspot.com

Then go and wash them—but quickly, because the soup is getting cold!"

The process would better be cyclical, meaning that after implementing no. 4/ we should start all over again and continue during the lifetime of the controlled process, hopefully not in flat circles but in progressive spirals.

The Controller could then be defined as the entity (person, organization, machine etc.) that focuses on a chosen object /subject, has a clear understanding of how it should look like (or function / perform i.e. what the desired result should be), determines how it actually looks like (functions / performs) and takes corrective action to converge the existing status with the desired status, within a clearly defined period of time.

As you may have guessed from the Motto, I believe that the First Controller appears to have been in all religions and cultures of divine nature. And it proved to be quite efficient, as it was complemented by the best Protector ever—our own internal fear of damnation.

Anyway, the controlling process seems simple, logical and achievable. To illustrate this, I will take a simple reality exercise, such as the boiling of an egg. The Chef will be appointed as Controller and his hired help will do the execution. The purpose of the controlled process would be obtaining a properly boiled egg, according to the expectation of the Chef (this could mean hard—or soft-boiled, with variations between the two extremes), within a maximum of 15 minutes. For implementing the process we have an egg, a cooking recipient, salt and water, and a heat source. First execution—the egg does not come as desired (either too soft or too hard). Corrective action: take another egg and adjust the process. For example if you tried boiling it in a frying pan you may notice that the egg is not properly covered with water and thus the result is... half yak! If you overlooked adding the salt it may happen that the egg brakes in the process, so again you have a failure (unpleasant shape and egg-white all over the water). So you keep on improving, until the Controller confirms the desired result.

As I have no intention to blame improper boiling of eggs in contemporary Europe for the moral decay and consequently the systemic crisis we face today, let's move on... by going back a little, to Root 3—the Provider, respectively the idea that excessive expectations from the State as Primary Provider is one of the roots for current distress. There is an increasing pressure from individuals towards public service and budgetary allocation, in terms of social and economic rights, culture and education, health and order and so on.

While becoming excessively generous to the beneficiaries, the State grows also increasingly demanding (even aggressive) towards the contributors. I believe it is much better for everyone in the long run that people re-direct their focus to the family and close circle of friends as Primary Provider, while encouraging the State to become more of a facilitator and Provider of last resort. Such an approach would bring back responsibility into our lives, beyond the Moneyteistic smokescreen that we worship now. If we expect everything to be provided to us by a collective self, we will soon live like in the Story of Nobody—you can read more about that in the next Chapter.

Similarly, while trying to identify who is actually assuming a Controller responsibility in the modern world, one might come to the same conclusion. We seem to have lost, as society, the self-consciousness and self-control over an ancient set of rules that refer to morality and common sense. You will find in this chapter more quotes than usual, for two simple reasons: the first is that they reflect very well this message and the second because they represent evidence that "we", in our collective wisdom, previously knew what was good for us, but somehow lost focus over time.

"Laws control the lesser man. Right conduct controls the greater one"—Chinese Proverb.

"Character is doing the right thing when nobody's looking. There are too many people who think that the only thing that's right is to get by, and the only thing that's wrong is to get caught."—J.C. Watts[19].

Society has delegated the Controller function to bureaucratic bodies with which regular people cannot directly and effectively intercede. Only indirectly, in the election process, voters may hope that their choice of rulers, based on coherent political platforms (sic!) will cascade down to the State apparatus, in an efficient manner.

Unfortunately, what we experience currently is not only the fact that reality if far from that, but it even seems to get worse every other year! The more complex the world becomes, the more demanding the administrative systems, the less effective the appointed Controllers prove to be! Sometimes it becomes obvious that they no longer have a real understanding of the object (or subject) which they are supposed to control. As a consequence, they cannot set reasonable target for the desired status or even

---

[19] American politician, former football player (born 1957)

determine properly what the existing status is! The first four pillars mentioned in the beginning of the chapter, as simple as they are, seem beyond the reach of State Controller nowadays...

We are flooded by probabilities, statistical data and averages that usually look as "real" as this:

"The average human has one breast and one testicle..."—Des MacHale[20].

We are however influenced in other ways, which we do not require or even expect, with behavioral, chemical, genetic and other new-age tools. Even the classic marketing has turned into an instrument of mass manipulation, in the era of Moneyteism and Consumerism.

The world has currently billions of systems functioning in parallel and at the same time interacting with each other, making it impossible to the mortal soul to see "the big image" anymore. Base processes are increasingly complex and efficient, and at the same time their controlling complements evolve into dangerously sophisticated ones. The problem with such systems is that they do not have intuition or morale, cannot act on hunch and cannot see when they are scammed in a non-conventional way. Everybody with a fair knowledge of how something is operated can easily cheat both the system and its controls.

"Know the rules well, so you can break them effectively"—Dalai Lama.

Unfortunately, this applies to all kinds of systems—both real physical ones (such as computers, machinery, technology, physics, bio-chemistry, and so on), but also to finance and taxation, social

---

[20] Irish Professor of Mathematics (born 1946)

welfare and education, health and culture, law and enforcement etc. The main question to be raised is how accurate and appropriate are the connectors between the base systems, the controllers, the protectors and the decision-makers.

What is actually lingering in the recent years on the financial and political scene is a proper understanding of the objects of controlling processes. The world leaders seem to fail to determine the very nature of the problems, in order to produce a solution or at least initiate steps in a reasonable direction. Perhaps this is also part of the failure equation: given current transparency and media exposure, too many minds are focused at the same time on too many big problems. Previously such crises were handled by a handful of people behind closed doors. Then the implementation was rather straight forward, as the systems were simpler and easier to handle, without collateral damage on other unforeseeable aspects.

On the other hand, not too many people appear to be working on small problems in good faith, with professionalism and enthusiasm. There is a great expectation placed on the generic systems, on the social and financial mechanisms, on the government intervention tools. People seem to have lost interest in doing their own ordinary daily jobs; they prefer to focus on debating and worrying how to solve the world's global problems.

When, how and why did this happen?

Well... it would really be childish to imagine that humanity could have been spared of overheating and miscommunication. When I was a child, we used to play a funny game called "wireless phone" (yes, back in the '70s!). We were sitting in a circle and one of the kids would start the communication by whispering something to the ear of the one sitting next to him/her. The recipient was then whispering to the next one and so on, until the last person in the circle was saying out loud the final message. We had great fun with this game, because it was always a huge difference between initial and final message.

Same breakdown in communication happened to the world and its controlling patterns. Understanding the object (or subject) of the controlling process is getting more difficult, the statistical measurements sometimes cannot transpose (or may even distort) the reality, the forecasting models seldom have the strength to actually predict future evolutions. Under current globalization context even the simplest translation of the same piece of legislation across different languages and cultures is sometime an insurmountable hurdle. More economists are channeling attention to behavioral economics, in an attempt to improve the predictability power of their models.

On the other end of the process, corrective measures cannot be contained only to the processes which they aim to improve, but are increasingly impacting on related processes, triggering chain effects really difficult to anticipate. I do not believe in a global conspiracy theory, for a simple reason: cannot imagine someone having control over so many variables, processes and interdependent systems. I do believe however in multiple local conspiracies, various alliances and regional influences, where a handful of people try to shift the power balance, at least temporary, in their favor. I also believe in the general rule that smaller fish is easily eaten by bigger one, but also in the random presence of a David or two—here and there.

With every new chapter, I feel like questioning the very idea that we are living a "crisis", but start wondering whether we are experiencing a purely systemic change, the beginning of a new global order. We need to be able to recognize this, then to understand how it works, so that in the end become ready to embrace and adapt to it.

The question is: where should we start from?

Why not seeking in this new context our own path to happiness and peace, health and prosperity? We might take small but steady steps toward improvement of our microenvironment, within the limits of decency and common sense. Because... "If you think you are too small to make a difference, try sleeping with a mosquito"— also Dalai Lama.

Therefore, I would extend such an invitation today, to everyone— friend or foe, supporter or critic. Re-shift your full attention to your own business—on both personal and professional level. Stop trying to solve global problems and focus instead on controlling your own circle of influence, providing for your own family and supporting your close community. Take the necessary steps to improve what you can and prepare yourself for doing this without help from external providential Providers or Controllers. Don't skip phases, never forget from where you started and do not let negativity kick you off-road from that good promising path that you have chosen.

I close the chapter with a dream about the Controller of the future—another quote that is actually a rule, which could be individually globalized if only...

"Rule #1: Use your good judgment in all situations. There will be no additional rules."

(Nordstrom's Employee Handbook)

ROOT 7—THE OTHER

Motto

The story of the four people named Everybody,
Somebody, Anybody and Nobody:
"There was an important job to be done and
Everybody was sure that Somebody would do it.
Anybody could have done it, but Nobody did it.
Somebody got upset about that, because it was
Everybody's job.
Everybody thought Anybody could do it, but Nobody
realized that Everybody wouldn't do it.
It ended up that Everybody blamed Somebody
when Nobody did what Anybody could have done."
(Source: largely available on Internet...)

This chapter's choice of root is quite a big challenge in terms of contributing something more than the motto, especially as the above wisdom (or leadership lesson) costs only some 10 euro in Hamburg, embedded on a nice metal plate.

Still, I will invest a little more time and words into it, to tackle the amplitude of "the other" approach to life, in the contemporary perception of reality. For this purpose, let's bring in another classic quote:

"Tomorrow is another day!"

Yes, it is!

And so was today yesterday, and now tomorrow is already gone...

Don't get me wrong, in that wonderful "Gone with the Wind" universe, this was a wise thing to say. Scarlett's approach can actually be used as a change driver, whenever time is needed to patiently take reasonable steps. However, the same four words taken out of context and used as an excuse for continuous postponement could induce a sense of procrastination.

I have come to regard "the other" as a root of many evils mostly because of the size of the phenomenon. There are two major aspects of this problem—the other regarded as a solution and the other taken as a benchmark. So let's take a deep dive now, starting with "the other" as a solution.

The idea that "it has to be done" is gaining ground over "I have to do it." The story of the four collective characters in the motto is only one dimension of "the other", two significant others being time and space, while we can even think of more applicable areas (such as cultures). The excuse for not doing something vary from "this would never work here" to "this is not the right time for it", going through "not my job"—classical drivers of "the other" approach.

We have become so reliant on the services that "the other" provides that we are gradually eroding our instincts of survival, self-preservation and responsibility. We have outsourced so many things in the name of comfort and efficiency, that we are swiftly becoming specialized in one thing only: getting through life as comfortable as possible. We have learned to expect things to happen, to be done, to get solved, regulated, enforced, and taken care of; and so on.

Civilized society has become a master at giving tasks and expecting perfect results, tending however to forget about the complexity and originality of people. There should be no surprise that the outcome is sometimes unpredictable, and not just a simple button-pushing-guaranteed-result-delivery-service.

Some people wake up in the morning just wishing (or better said expecting) that things which interfere with their daily comfort or involve long-term-hard-work-responsibility would be taken care somehow by "the other". They idealize money as the answer to all the problems (as a way to pay for the service), therefore get frustrated when "the other" can externalize more, as they have more money.

And so I get to "the other" as a benchmark. Humans are socially ambitious creatures, inclined to compare themselves to the better performing members of the community. Some even experience a sense of satisfaction from being "above" the less fortunate, while still looking out for the ones who are doing better. In this process they no longer pause to enjoy life as it is, because of constantly comparing to "the other", while the secret of happiness is not only about getting something (or someone, or somewhere), but mostly about still wanting it afterwards. And that is very hard when one always compares...

What is then left after delegating regular life to others, in order to free time and keep on running after imaginary "others" who are doing eternally better?

Have you noticed how often people complain about not having enough personal time left for real living? But when they actually manage to get spare time, as they do not need it for petty little things anymore (yes—those are already done better by others!), some start wondering about the real purpose of life. Funny enough, in the end, people leaving within continuously shifting reference systems, would either get bored of having too much time, or burned-out by working too hard on a job that has nothing to do with their own passion in life, even though it was supposed to pay for allowing the passion into their life... Confusing, isn't it?!

Have you ever wondered why is it so hard to do certain things ourselves, but easily expect others to do them instead? Why is it difficult to change things that are directly or indirectly related to us, no matter whether we talk about small or big things, affecting our intimate environment? Why the same "we" that cannot initiate change within us are always so ready, willing and determined to change THE OTHERS? Why we expect them to immediately come closer to what we expect, molding to fit our image of the ideal "them"? Why we always forgive ourselves for not being able to change, but we find it hard to forgive others for not becoming who we want them to be?

Sorry for the avalanche of questions, but this topic has a way of storming my neurons and raising my blood pressure like no other!

There could be many answers as I could think, in no particular order, about comfort, selfishness, human nature, expectations about roles in society, rights and duties, misperception about means and results, drivers and motivation for change. It is always easier to recognize mistakes or shortcomings in others before we admit them within ourselves.

Ideally, we may wish to transform others out of a selfless desire to help them. We learn from own experience and then try to teach also the others, in an attempt to prevent them from hurting themselves in a similar way. Still, we tend to forget about their own circle of comfort and resistance to change, and then we get disappointed when failing to influence. In my professional life, I have empirically established that banks can never restructure a borrower against its wish. They should not even try, as it always turns out both expensive and futile. The same applies to regular life—no one could transform a person unless that person wants it and has already acceded to such motivation that might trigger the change from within.

In the end, let's also recognize that the biggest catalyst for "the other" symptom is the constantly growing offer of such available others. Communities are getting bigger, while we feel smaller and more insignificant every day. We know that we cannot change the world, so why should we even bother?

Yes, the others are protecting our comfort! But they are also preventing our change, at the same time. We have grown to need them so much, that we do not know how to live independent of them anymore!

So, should we do anything at all about this? Or just accept it as an evolutionary treat of an increasingly artificially intelligent (sic!) world?

I cannot speak for the others, but I for one plan to start taking back some of those things already given away... How much? Hopefully enough to preserve myself into my life!

ROOT 8—THE WASTE

Motto:
"The gap in our economy is between what we have and what we think we ought to have—and that is a moral problem, not an economic one."

Paul Heyne[21]

The ferociousness of this root suddenly hit me about one year after the start of the series, while I was going through the motions of my morning routine, preparing for a new sunny summer day.

The motto comes from a great guy whose biography on the Wikipedia is not as long as he would deserve. He was a modest but extremely wise fighter in a war that we should all enroll in, if we wish to remodel our world for a better future: Paul Heyne strived to inspire morality to a certain age segment, where he believed he could induce the greatest change—adolescence. He had both theological and economical background and dedicated his life to teaching youngsters how to best combine the elementary principles of these two areas in making day-to-day choices, coming up with a kind of morally-driven economics.

---

[21] American economist and lecturer, author of the book 'The economic way of thinking' (1931–2000)

He reminds me of my mother.

She used to teach social sciences in high school, which included economics, philosophy and political studies back in the communist period. Same as Heyne, she chose to work with undergraduates, even thus university career was also tempting, better paid and with higher recognition.

There were of course notable differences, as he lived in the capitalist Seattle while she was struggling in the communist Bucharest, they had distinctive focus areas and methods of teaching. However, the impact on young people's destiny was rather similar—guidance through hormonal storms and vanity races, thus shaping kids into beautiful promising adults.

The common way in which they managed to achieve that was by combining tools from different areas of culture and science but, most important, life. Anyone sitting in their classrooms would embark in a journey of philosophical stories, language games, social and economic challenges packed with examples from the literary world, ethical and moral challenges sometimes touching also religious aspects. Heyne's theological background made his use of the latest more obvious, while my mother strived to display a more liberal approach, as in the communist period the religion was taboo.

They were both strong individuals that immersed selflessly in the act of teaching, sharing the best part of their knowledge to everyone who was eager to learn. And that proved to be enough for most of their students, and the result was obvious. I still remember chance encounters in the street, when I was still a child and my mother's path would cross with former scholars. Those people that came out of her molding hands where greatly accomplished individuals, with good moral standing and healthy family lives. And they would always stop not only to say "hello", but to try and concentrate in a couple of minutes' conversation what otherwise would need hours to share, if only we had the time!... They would manage to catch up on things in one breath and then thank her for all the great lessons and memorable words still deeply engraved in their hearts, and lived by—every day!

Paul Heyne also gave to the world a valuable book, called "The economic way of thinking", popular amongst ex-communist audience, including Romania. He had a pragmatic and at the same time critical approach regarding the conflicting views of "classic" economic doctrines, blaming the lack of proper communication and the excessive theoretical inclination of the economists for this divergence (with good reason, in my opinion!).

Coming back to the topic at hand, the choice of the motto was quite a challenge, as there were so many great one on this topic. Here are the other finalists:

He who buys what he does not need steals from himself (Author Unknown).

The hardest thing is to take less when you can get more (Kin Hubbard).

Growth for the sake of growth is the ideology of the cancer cell (Edward Abbey).

Indeed, humankind's inclination towards waste is one of its biggest weaknesses! It took me one year to actually notice and include it in the roots, probably because I live with it every day! Even though recognizing it should make me strong enough to overcome it, such a powerful enemy still gets the best of me far too often...

That summer morning it just hit me—how much it has spread like a cancer, invading our way of living, getting so used to it that we are not aware any longer of the damage it actually does.

The trigger for my understanding this may seem strange, but it happened while opening a simple ordinary new pack of toilet paper—nice and pink, slightly scented. And suddenly a big part of my childhood started to unroll before my eyes...

Just like magic, I was transported back to my home town in Bucharest, sometimes in the 80s, when the toilet paper was also pink, but not so soft and funny scented. It was sold in bookstores next to other paper products and was a very scarce resource. Just like food and electricity and a lot of other things which we now take for granted. We used to be very careful how much we use and we actually had a lot of jokes about alternatives to toilet paper—will not bore you with details.

Basically this is how we managed to overcome the scarcity of resources back then—with humor and a lot of love. We were happy and valued everything in a different way. Bananas were shared between me and my sister and I can hardly remember my parents having any. Cakes were made in house once or twice a week, as sugar was rationalized per person (controlled, but healthy policy!). We were always sharing with our neighbors, nice old ladies with great skills for sweets-producing, who would also share their cakes with us. Pop-corn was the result of team work for preparing and we had a special supply of it, being very popular in the neighborhood because of that.

Culinary activities were carefully planned (as gas was also scarce), and food variety optimized by the "cooking-time" criteria. On special occasions we would indulge with oven-prepared meals and other "fire intensive" specialties. Heating was confined to the "winter rooms" and the kitchen was quite an adventure for my mother in cold season, but she managed it with love and dignity, while results were always tasty, as she never compromised on quality.

My father was also occasionally cooking, and he was the "bad boy" of the family in this respect. He never liked rationalizing—either raw materials or time. Therefore, he used to display two or three culinary books when he was "creating", and only optimized the tasty outcome! This is probably why my sister and I had so much fun whenever he performed one of those acts...

Smiling back on those times, I believe that the variety and at the same time scarcity that was blended by our parents into our daily meals ensured the healthy growth of both our bodies and minds.

Clothing was mended with love and care, passed on from older to younger siblings, always clean and sometimes transformed, so it wouldn't look the same. Soap was fabricated in house for washing clothes and was an excellent disinfectant (good for hair-washing also). We were raising hens in our courtyard and they were gracefully giving "natural" eggs in return. I remember those birds that were growing too old to be eaten and were considered as family members anyway... except for our dog, who could not accept being associated with such funny creatures, so was chasing them around (in good faith!), just to demonstrate who the boss was...

In school, apart from the standard subjects, we were also learning basic housing skills (cooking and sewing) and we created really nice things that are most probably still stashed somewhere in the attic. It was a wonderful childhood and I can't help comparing this to contemporary life.

Creativity is encouraged today in every school, with even wider choices that back then. However the abundance of disposable things is gradually eating up many hard-working ways of collecting memories. It is difficult to choose a favorite doll when you have tens of them, or to look forward to eating your half of a banana, while your parents are begging you to eat healthy from hundreds of options.

We should be very careful about providing too much for our young ones, as anyhow the older we get, the more we are swept into the waste tornado. Some of us have already been swallowed by it in our daily personal lives, others in our professional lives, while many of us in both. Some give in to this temptation on daily basis, and some less frequently, but with bigger collateral damage!

So… what exactly do I have in mind under this "waste" label?

First of all, buying too much food and using too much paper then throwing it away, getting the newest and most technologically advanced piece of equipment and discarding the good old one, while it is still fully functional. Then we have the myriad of single use products on the shelf, which are there to ensure continuous sales for their manufacturers, going beyond those officially labeled as such—there are "long-term" things that break immediately after their warranty expires, just because they were not really designed to last!

We have billions of options in terms of cosmetics, clothing, accessories, food, medicine, cars and IT gadgets. I wonder what happens to those who are not chosen to come home with us or to those that we buy just to put on some shelf and never use, which we finally throw away (or in the best case donate to some charity that proves to be another business that introduces them in second hand stores from distant countries, waiting again for someone to take them home...).

And then there are billions of residential, office and commercial square meters which are being built as you read this, to add to the offer of already vacant billions of residential, office and commercial spaces that wonder if they would ever be chosen by the less and less wealthy ordinary people, as well as by the less and less successful middle-sized firms.

We buy unnecessary stuff from businesses which over-expand, counting on their product being better than the competitors, but then killing each other in the process, as the prices go down for everybody.

But one of the worst kinds of waste is that of our creativity, blown away by a civilization creating robots, surrogates of live and substitutes for brain, disregarding the fact that our humanity only emerges at the intersection of body and soul.

Several years ago I was sitting in a bus in Bucharest, next to a kid and a young man. The kid was talking about the most recent movie he had seen and the guy next to him asked:

"When did you last read a book?"

The kid looked confused and struggled to give an answer, about how it was easier and more entertaining to see a movie. Then the guy said:

"Yes, that is true. But a movie will never give you what a book can. In a movie you only see a very narrow world, which the director imagined for himself and wanted to reveal to the public. When you read a book you can imagine things the way you like, in the colors you choose, and you can make the character as beautiful or as ugly as you wish. In a book you read with your own mind and feel with your own soul, therefore build your own world; while in a movie you are just a passive observer of someone else's world."

I wished there were microphones in that bus and the creativity lesson coming from a young (but wise) man would be broadcasted on all TV channels during prime time. Unfortunately it was something unlikely to happen in this world, as we were already programmed to waste that prime time with negative news, turning us into passive observers of a manipulative view of world events.

Modern communication channels molded people into correlated automatic answering machines, triggered by certain stimulus which the owners of such network orchestrate—negative, panicking, gloomy, "global-crisis-self-fulfilling-future-losers". It is indeed a waste of our creative, positive, loving, solution-oriented and long-term surviving selves.

What else do we waste, apart from material things and spiritual potential?

Basically we experience a huge waste of our otherwise very limited... TIME!

We spend it nowadays in so many funny ways that do not enhance our spirituality. Let's take for example politics. In the good old days when media was not so wide-spread, this used to be a necessary evil of the organized society. A handful of people were paid from contributor's money to spend their time playing political games with a reasonable outcome, which I suspect was to preserve some ground rules and proper order in the community. Nowadays, apart from the fact that the purpose of the politicians is not very clear anymore, we also have another systemic problem: every citizen with voting right is now wasting time on politics! Nothing more needs to be said, readers should know already why I would categorize this as a total waste... And we pay very much for this, much more than we can even begin to imagine.

Not to mention that the term "politics" does not necessarily refer to State issues, but touches a much wider area of our life—we have to act political at work, in our personal circle, sometimes even at home. A reasonable part of this politics might bring good and positive result; however making it the main driver of our daily reality would really turn it into a big waste. As with everything else in life, finding the right balance is a challenge.

I could go on forever about various forms of waste, but then become guilty of the movie director sin—imposing my view on the story and thus stopping your imagination from running wild. I bet you can come up with huge number of examples of your own, so please do so!

To wrap this up, let's pick this root question: how come we slide so easy from scarcity to waste?

In case of the ex-communist countries the change was swift, in the advanced economies the transition happened slower. In some countries the scarcity is still there and it is another proof of the cancer-like problems in our world, as there is a lack of will and determination to put global waste to a good use and help those who suffer.

Otherwise, transition from scarcity to wealth and further to waste, is part of human nature, essentially connected to the need for comfort and security. This was originally a good and desirable evolution, if only we knew when and where to draw the line before turning to waste.

Perhaps the ascension of this trouble-maker, rooted into temptation, has to do with the fact that the world has become a huge consumption-driven mechanism. Behavioral economics, a rather recent concept amongst other economic sciences, is all about revealing how our faulty human nature rules our choices, how marketing degenerated into manipulation, and how silly we can behave when facing our own weaknesses, and being addressed with the right temptation ("right" meaning a mix of dosage, place and time plus, as someone said it so nice, lack of witnesses!...).

More than that, financing products have recently disconnected our purchasing power from real net worth (and, more sadly, also from social and health insurance schemes!), creating a bubble exactly from what the motto points out: it made some of our dreams become possible even when they shouldn't have!

It is nothing wrong with dreaming, as long as we can still discern between dream and reality. Unfortunately, the good old sense of responsibility and accountability got diluted in this process and people took what they thought they deserved without wondering who would pay for this in the end. Unfortunately the bill will be paid by all of us and even our children, unless they rebel and refuse to endorse the waste created by their "old folks".

Therefore, with the risk of repeating myself, I will say it once again: we are not living a crisis, but a paradigm shift, something that happens almost every century, a transformation which will give birth to a new world. For better or for worse—this remains yet to be seen.

I hope we have grown wiser at least in the way that we should not shed blood for cleaning ourselves this time, while we may still do it with water, soap and self-control! And there are at least a couple of good news, when we glimpse into the ways ahead.

First of all, it looks like not everyone has given into the temptation of waste; there are clusters of morally healthy people everywhere, raising beautiful kids; there are also beautiful teachers still fighting for the integrity of our future generations.

Second, this is one global problem for which no global resources need to be identified! We can and need to tackle it individually, within ourselves, our families and our closest circles. It is at the same time difficult, because this challenges everyone to become personally responsible for their own choices.

However it is exactly where our hope for the future lies—waking up, re-shaping our dreams and re-assessing our behavior according also to our resources, both material and spiritual, as individuals but also social-wise. We should then bring back the common sense into our lives, and go in search of a long-lasting sense of satisfaction, which lately got lost in the race for easy superficial pleasure.

ROOT 9—THE RISK TAKER

Until recently, I did not see myself as a risk taker, but a rather conservative person with established habits, reasonable expectations and fears, balanced by a prudential nature. But as time went by, I started to notice in my approach to life an inclination to predictive hazard management—building a safety net, by taking small risks on a daily basis. I was just calling them actions, decisions, and choices—impulsive or wise steps forward, or sideways (or even backward sometimes), generating inherent consequences.

Next thing I observed was that my attitude towards decision-making was different when dealing with personal challenges as compared to professional ones.

More specifically, in the private life I might take actions that could hurt me, for the sake of various arguments—basically connected to feelings, preferences, personal comfort and moral principles. The approach on professional life is far more prudent and cautious, as most decisions have impact on others. Therefore, rationale and objective filters come first (such as economic and legal correlations, statistics and market data, experience etc.), premises need to be challenged and data sources verified, and only then I become ready to elaborate alternative scenarios. In the end, those also need to pass the subjective–affective–empathy test, with consideration for the people involved.

There are many points of convergence between those two ways, as they are built around similar ethical principles (whoever[22] said there was no business ethics but just ethics was right!), resulting approach being just a little more conservative in my case whenever decisions are deemed to impact third party interests (money, career, and life in general).

One cold morning in the early 2013, when I first thought about the difference, I was enjoying a hot cup of coffee with one of my professional mentors. While exploring this, a question popped up:

"Do you think this is normal?"

Lucky for me, he understood very well, admitting to (re)acting basically the same, even though he said it seemed like a joke played on us by nature. Darwin would definitely turn in his grave seeing how both of us contradict his basic thesis, meaning humans were supposed to be self-protective and fight for survival under the most adverse conditions, not the other way around, self-destructive and protective with others.

---

[22] John C. Maxwell (bestselling author, coach, and speaker on leadership topics), in his book 'There's no such thing as "Business Ethics"'

Unfortunately, building a successful career nowadays mostly requires self-focus, presenting favorably your own results (or sometimes even assuming others"), hiding problems and avoiding conflicts that would compromise the possibility of promotion. What we were discussing was exactly the opposite—the need of capable visionary people, who would be able to identify potential problems timely and accurately, solve them efficiently and bring long-term benefits to the organization. We both preferred strong characters that would assume consequence of their actions, even if in the short run such approach could jeopardize career plans.

About the same time I was watching a BBC World round table[23] with effective turnaround managers. The participants had a few things in common, amongst which genuine curiosity and practical grasp on things, plus a similar (fascinating!) risk taking profile—their own image and survival as managers did not weight more than doing the "right thing" for the companies they serviced!

The next week the same TV channel broadcasted another story, of yet similar character. All those success stories (be it national post or royal railway company) were similar—complex deeply troubled situations, which needed drastic and unpopular measures. Those men invited at the helm during difficult times were hated by the employees and trashed by entire local media, back when they needed to drive the change. And then, 10 years down the road, they were regarded as geniuses and a world in crisis was seeking their advice during prime time on BBC!

---

[23] 'The Bottom Line' cycle hosted by Evan Davis, on a Sunday edition with 3 turnaround managers—Adam Crozier (ex-CEO / Royal Mail), James Eden (Owner & CEO/ Private White) and Nick Sanders (portfolio manager / Better Capital).

Their most important messages were that first you have to stop pretending everything is fine; then you should be enthusiastically curious and ask the right questions to the right people (which are usually not the ones at the top of the company), to get to the root of the problems; then you just need to correlate and act. One of the most interesting things one of them said was that usually the lower management knew exactly what was wrong within the organization, but could not point to a way out. It was natural, as solutions could only come from the top, after correlating causes and deciding on a strategy. Because without knowing which way to go, no improvement could be achieved!

That evening I went to bed with a smile and a peaceful sense of being on the right path.

Next week-end I came across a CNN broadcast, again with experienced guests, this time talking about the financial crisis. One of the participants presented her view—about why banks should not be blamed for the excessive lending. She said that in case the bank offered financing for a house or a project which you, as a borrower, knew you would not afford to repay, it was your moral responsibility to say "no" to that bank. She also said that the guilt should be at least shared between the banks and the society, as it is not only about mistakes of some lender giving away too much money without proper assessment, but also about individuals and companies which were knowingly signing on loans they knew they would not be able to repay.

The truth may be, as always, somewhere in the middle. One should not have taken too much; the other should not have given. And the main trigger was most probably the changing perception of front office bankers about banking, which gradually became a reward-driven sales business, with a rather easy task—giving money to people who did not have enough!

And there is one flaw that the Controllers of the financial market either overlooked or underestimated: a well-intended separation of tasks that disconnected the sales and the risk functions, designed to prevent hazardous lending, indirectly diluted the responsibility for getting the money back (see also the story of nobody—the Motto of Root 7). Basically, the banker was motivated to lend as much as possible without much concern about what happens at maturity, while the customer was anyway trying to get as much money as possible, without much concern about how it will be paid back. So, why are we still surprised of what happened? As of today, the huge volumes of non-performing loans had not been absorbed yet by the market and the Controllers are still looking for solutions to squeeze an over-inflated Gennie back in the bottle...

Without further exploring the "blame" logic, I just refer you to the previous root (The Waste) and our human nature, inclined to buy more than we need and often even more than we can consume. It is a predictable behavior that sales and marketing are based upon, the latter scientifically gaining such a manipulative power that can easily induce false needs these days.

Universal banks' inclination towards consumer-oriented lending in the last decades has to do more with pure selling (products, promises, dreams...) than financial advice, so it seems not much different from clothing, energy drinks or electronics. Even more, it has one intrinsic characteristic which makes it the most powerful and dangerous of all the consumer products—the lending "product" can be mentally associated with (and exchanged for) any real one already aggressively marketed, thus multiplying its penetration rate a thousand times.

Advertising, hand in hand with Moneyteistic gods that replaced classic heroes in our contemporary society also induce an artificially inflated need of money. Just plug your bank's product to the idea of shopping or housing or exotic holiday or whatever is trending on the market and... here you go, you have a loan! I remember an advertisement back in 2008: "If you cannot afford a house don't be sad, we can lend you the money!" Right! How about affording both the interest and the house price in this case?!

Finally, to complicate matters even more, financial market became excessively fragmented and competitive, meaning that there will always be an alternative for someone in need of a loan. Bad debtors just migrate to the weakest entry point in the system. Therefore, the most frequent question addressed to the banks after bubbles break ("Why did you give them the money?") is actually a hoax—if not that one, it would have been another, as debtors always find someone willing to lend, in the crazy race for market share.

Unfortunately I also believe that moral hazard in banks has not peaked yet, as the Big Provider (i.e. the State) guarantees higher deposit volumes every year and the banks feel free to act riskier, as they remain liable mostly towards equity and bond holders, with less social bearing than individual depositors. So, the snowball keeps on rolling, while the virtual money keeps on multiplying...

Anyway, let's come back to the topic at hand today—the risk taking.

Risk assessment is involved in every decision in our life. For every choice there are alternatives and for each alternative a risk-return (or risk-result) judgment must be passed. Individuals have unique decision-making mechanisms, which translates into lower or higher risk taking profiles—between recklessness and adversity being an infinite number of possibilities.

I will use an over-simplified classification today, in a rather extreme manner, while assuming the consequence that its relevance would be limited. The scope of this exercise is to assist the readers in assessing their own profile, as well as explore others' with whom they interact, personally or professionally. The classification I am about to design is based on the risk analysis behind the decisions we make and starts from the following premise: frequently, when people consider they "do the right thing", they usually act in pursuit of their own interest. Therefore, correct understanding of respective interest has an essential role in calibration of the decision process, as well as in the negotiation with others.

I will use the two characteristics already identified in the beginning of this chapter—the attitude towards those risks affecting the self vs. those affecting others. I would then group the people as per their self-protective vs. others-protective actions, while the degree of manifested care can vary from indifferent to over-protective.

First, there are the genuine risk-adverse folks. They permanently think (if taken to the extreme—too much!) about protecting both themselves and others around them, sometimes passing good opportunities and ignoring basic needs, because of their fear of failure. They live their life apparently safe, away from the dangers of a nasty world. They are most likely not among those who triggered the crisis, but may very well be a large part of the victims, after placing their life savings in "safe" investments... and as one of the basic flaws of the current banking systems is that it uses the "multiplication" approach on all types of financing sources, when the risk-adverse folks use banking services for managing their cash (salary, deposits etc.), they unknowingly become risk-takers, as their money is used to leverage the entire system.

Second, we have the self-protective folks that do not care much about protecting others. Those people ready and willing to take almost any risk as long as it does not negatively reflect on themselves (either in terms of money or other resources, image, comfort, or security…). If we look upon the outcome of their actions, on the positive side of the spectrum we may find some genius entrepreneurs or charismatic leaders, who manage to build exceptionally successful businesses. In the middle we may find regular people or silly day-dreamers (who don't take much action because other do not entrust them with their resources). On the negative side of the spectrum we find thieves, criminals and crooks. There are famous movies about this character profile, usually the story of success that came out of nothing ("don't ask about the first one million…" kind of tales), but also a lot of bad-loan borrowers actually fit into this profile. One of the most hazardous situations comes whenever this type of character benefits of a legitimate personal gain scheme directly connected to the level of risk taking they can advise—the classical debate about misuse of bonus schemes in the financial world.

Third, we have the "hero" profile, respectively the self-destructive (or self-careless or at the very best the self-neutral) folks, who care about protecting other people. Some of them made history, others just died anonymously throughout our history. I read once a practical psychology book[24] where I found an interesting theory—that we may be genetically predisposed towards paranoia, inherited from our ancestors. The authors were saying that the brave and fearless heroes usually died young with little time and chances to generate a succession line, while the prudent and paranoid ones lived longer life and had bigger families, with descendants in our days.

Fourth, we have the absolute dummies, those who do not care either about themselves or about others. I strongly hope this is a rare species, as they either hurt themselves really early in life and migrate to any of the other categories or become purely medical cases and we don't see them too often walking freely among us... so I will not insist on those folks.

Finally, we have a "reasonable mix" risk-taking profile, stretching across all the above four categories, in a moderate manner. Here I include those people who combine a healthy self-protective profile with a good sense of responsibility for protecting others. People who fall in this category take decently calculated risks and assume the consequences of their decisions.

Ideally, most of the active population should fit into the last category. Practically, I still wonder on a daily basis... Actually, there is a fine border between those over-simplified types of risk takers. As I mentioned at the beginning of this exercise, the simplification and generalization takes away a lot of relevance, but I still believe it is a useful tool for opening the path to debate. In real life, an individual would most likely present variable reactions according to diverse types of risks at different moments, under circumstantial position influenced also by relationships involved.

_____

[24] F. Lelord & C. Andre—How to manage difficult personalities (French 'Comment Gèrer les Personalites Difficilès')

In the professional environment too little importance is given to psychological profiling—both when existing staff is assisted to design career plans and when companies recruit new staff. Instead, there is much weight put on education (not knowledge!), monetary and status considerations, both on the side of the applicants and the recruiters. Schooling priorities on the other hand are frequently set by family or driven by community expectations, directing youngsters towards jobs that pay well or offer quick growth prospects. When reaching maturity, some find themselves trapped between own dreams, social pressure, and a questionable compromise already made, in an attempt to fit into models that don't really suit them.

Psychological profiling could address many issues, from ethical principles and moral standards to aptitudes and talents. It should be encoded both in the educational system and in later career planning. And for those professions that are highly exposed to risk taking and moral hazard, such tests should be a prerequisite not only on managerial, but even on entry level. I know it sounds like utopia, but we have to start thinking outside the box if we wish to make things better for our children. Just because young graduates may be good with numbers does not guarantee that they do not get out of universities with the mind-set of a crook. Technical background is not enough to succeed in a sustainable way, not if we want to put the trust back into the financial system.

And anyway, the same conclusion could apply to almost any industry, even if the financial world is mostly under scrutiny. It is only natural to always be in the spotlight, as it runs through the entire system and connects all other areas, just like the blood inside the body. Still, it is definitely not the only one corrupted by moral hazard. Food and trading, sports and entertainment, politics and social service, research and education, health and drugs—if you would follow the news you would soon understand that the ethical roots of current crisis are widely spread throughout every area in our life.

If I was to put together what I have learned in the past few years (be it from industry turnaround managers, financial gurus, famous journalists or striving regulators), it seems that we are running in circles. The world is trying to put more technical rules into various systems which are actually sinking because of moral hazard and excessive risk taking, personal gain and creative data manipulation.

The approach is partially correct, but unfortunately incomplete. Whenever new and more restrictive regulations come into a market, it takes its main players probably around 6 to 12 months to re-adjust to those rules, by introducing new controls and adapting the statistics they generate, without actually changing anything in their core processes. The automotive gas emission scandal was one of the most eloquent examples of this kind; however similar situations on smaller scale (or deeper underground) are present all over the world.

The core (dis)functionalities of any market where there is a need for tougher regulation can only be addressed by going beyond the rules and technical standards, by appointing individuals that have the capacity to transform their organizations. Any change that remains on paper may induce dangerous gaps between formal and informal, reality and pretense. Breaking the vicious circle will only become possible when the Controllers will focus on the key people in the systems, bringing to public attention both success stories and lessons learned.

Our systems are in urgent need of turnaround managers, capable and willing to assume responsibility, identify the problems and take all the necessary steps for solving them in a sustainable way, for the benefit of a global market. Nobody should wish for a collapse in the financial system before having created something functional to replace what we currently have—unless we have nothing against going back several hundred years, and probably fight some nasty wars in between.

How should we change?

By encouraging capable and courageous people to wisely take temporary risk of personal failure whenever they have a clear vision of a long-term common benefit...

By understanding that lessons-learned should not be immediately turned into finger-pointing, but instead be given reasonable time to lay foundation for future success-stories...

And by doing all that... even sooner than possible!

ROOT 10—THE COMMUNICATION

Brain waves. Hugs. Signs. Words.

Papyrus. Paper. Morse. Feather. Coal. Chalk. Pen. Keyboard. Touch screen.

Music. Dance. Sculpture. Painting. Building. Flying...

Pigeon. Horse. Post. Courier. Internet. Email. Call. Sms. Chat.

Theatre. Opera. Multiplex.

Radio. Tv. Computer. Phone.

Evolution or involution? Curse or blessing?

Fear or desire? Irony or smile? Tear or laughter?

Love or hate? Acceptance or rejection? Hurt or embrace? Anticipation or avoidance?

Honesty or deceit? Reality or dream?

Photo or paint? Live or unplugged?

Eloquent or ambiguous? Intimate or public? Gentle or aggressive?

Build or destroy? Divide or join? Break or conquer?

Manipulate or convince? Seek or avoid? Share or hide?

Give or take? Endorse or disclaim?

Listen or hear? Watch or see? Say or insinuate?

Loud or whispery? Stereo or surround?

Read or heard? Seen or imagined?

Flat or curved? Colored or b&w? Sepia?

Touch. Hold. Hug. Kiss. Weep. Smile. Frown. Laugh. Blink.

Speak. Feel. Smell. Hear. Taste.

Morning. Lunch. Afternoon. Evening. Night. Late at night. Early morning.

Clock.

Tick-tack.

Life.

Over and out.

By now I have already communicated to you more than in all previous nine roots put together. This would be true in case you have been reading properly each line and everything lying between and behind those lines. If you haven't, I invite you to slooowly read them again.

Did you find different meanings? Did you imagine different scenes and different persons on the second reading?

That could be triggered by the common but abstract nature of those words. We go through life convinced that we listen, understand and react. Actually we may very well spend most of our life imagining, translating and acting on what we think we know.

I believe that current communication patterns represent one of the deepest roots for the current global status of our world and I can think of many reasons for this correlation. One motive could be that we started to take too many (fake) things and news for granted. We are used to excess information, on so many levels and coming to us in so many packages that we are gradually turning off old-fashioned talks, as well as ignore our intuitive side. We (ab)use surrogate interaction and are gradually convinced that we know it all. We get carried away by online presence of hundreds of remote friends, adrenaline rush of movie characters, news about public persons, accomplishments of sportsmen and emotions of artists, most of them happening on a flat cold computer or television screen, while we are comfortably snoozing on some couch. We are nicely fitting in pre-packed life stories and consume enormous fake-data supply just as it is being fed to us. Quantity seems to have won the war over quality and is now taking heads-on another challenge: our time.

Some of us even got used to the idea that robots and people have daily access to our personal life and don't even bother about it anymore. A handful is fighting to win back the right to intimacy, but the 007 Genie is out of the bottle for a long time, on a planetary scale. One can only hope that the paranoia of supervised communication may actually have positive consequences, such as bringing back into our life that primary channel which matters the most: eye to eye. One can dream that someday we will go back to using all our given senses at the same time (including common sense!) and therefore minimize as much as possible further misunderstanding.

I wonder what else is to be said as a closing note. At this point it would be better just to challenge you to recall any classic French movie, and draw your own conclusions. When I was young I used to hate the fact that those movies had no ending. Today I would just turn off the set and move on, smiling upon the opened possibilities.

Life has revealed to me that one should not seek immediate answers to all the questions. Some things, facts and people are just there for reasons that would uncover much later in the process. Some events just happen, apparently for no reason. Demanding answers or closure beforetime might lead to misunderstanding of a much bigger picture that lies far away somewhere, apparently in the background...

INTERMEZZO

Up to now I shared with you a personal understanding on a global paradigm shift affecting all the aspects of our life, and a critical view of the roots leading here—the world being dominated by wrong priorities and questionable habits, dysfunctionality degenerating into crisis, and misunderstanding escalated to conflict.

I peeked behind our social masks and reflected on what we have become—slaves of our contradictory human nature: beautiful but ugly, free but selfish, intelligent but corrupted, talented but resentful, creative but erratic, virtuous but immoral, hospitable but intolerant, and so on...

I challenged you to reflect upon the possibility that each of us as an individual, and even more as a global community, must assume at least part of the blame for the world that we have created.

Now, it seems the right time to ask: are we really as helpless and hopeless as we seem to be? Are we just witnesses of a contemporary apocalypse, condemned to endless poverty, and being a passive subject in a manipulation scenario designed by someone else, somewhere out there?...

As far as I am concerned, with every root I explored, the need to search for reasons grew less acute and I started to stall writing, with good excuse, of course—frequent travelling, urgent tasks, late working hours... but then, all of a sudden, one fine evening, in the middle of this crazy running around through my own life, I stopped to wonder: why I am in such a hurry, whereto and to reach?... what—the end?... why do I dedicate so much time and energy, in search of... really, what am I actually searching for?!...

After collecting seven roots, I started that same evening a new series, in parallel. This one is looking forward, in search of a better future. And so, the next pages are all about... the WAYS!

PART II—Ways

WAY 1—THE MIRROR

Motto:
"What we are is God's gift to us, what we become is our gift to God."

Eleanor Powell

James Thurber[25] believed that "All men should strive to learn before they die what they are running from, and to, and why."

I was very young when I first came across that phrase and, even though his message looked wise, it felt really abstract at the same time. Then, one summer evening in 2012, I had a distinctive feeling of getting close to a tentative answer for the first part, namely the "running from" part. The rest of it still needed some serious exploration, as it was not only more difficult, but also highly volatile.

My grandmother used to make fun of the fact that her sleeping time got shorter as she got older (obviously not affecting her impressive energy level!). She always ended up saying: "Well, what

---

[25] James Thurber (1894–1961) was an American journalist, cartoonist & humorist, and writer (mostly playwrights—Broadway comedy); he lost one eye in a playing accident in his childhood, and later on became almost entirely blind, however continued his work with overwhelming success

can I do? I get up and get on with my life, as I will sleep long enough after I'm gone!"

While sleeplessness seems to be quite a common condition amongst the elderly, her attitude about it still touches me on a very personal level, as I connect now Thurber's questions with her wisdom. Once we have all the answers, we might as well stop running and just give in to that last, long sleep...

There was a hot Saturday, back in the summer of 2012, when I went out with some friends on a wine tasting trip, somewhere in the Southern Romania. We left our dear crowded capital really early in the morning and returned only late at night.

We experienced extreme heat out in the fields, beautifully integrated by one of our hosts into the story of his vineyard, a tale about people, grapes and survival under difficult weather conditions. Quality wine is all about passion for work and mutual respect, understanding and loving communion between men and nature. It may sound silly and outdated in this computerized world; however the magic of the place and the enthusiasm of the guy were convincing enough to make me feel part of something that will endure against any global crisis, local politics or cultural prejudices.

The story-teller of this adventure was a young Austrian who came to Romania some years before, hired as an expert consultant by the owners, to educate local workers in the spirit of efficiency and quality. Soon after arrival, instead of teaching those old fellows what he had theoretically learned back in school, he started to pay attention to their practical wisdom and decided to qualify himself on the job instead. Then he met another outlander and married her, and they both integrated perfectly in a community of hard workers with great hearts and skillful hands, working the fields and organizing touristic escapes, spiced with Romanian food and wine stories that fascinate us, large city workaholics.

He told us all about the specific needs of the plants, how they protect themselves under tough weather (drought, flooding or freeze). We learned how important it is to identify suitable land for each species, what is the right time for different activities and how much the harvest quality depends on the way the humans take good care of everything.

I will just mention two specific approaches, as they were quite different when compared to the vineyards around and the modern way of doing things: how the plant is cut, respectively watered.

The guy said he only cuts little bits of the plant, the purpose being just shedding away lifeless part and not at all trying to control its length. There were two reasons for this: first was that top leaves are the ones that protect the grapes (by maintaining shadow on sunny days, while acting as a natural umbrella on rainy ones), second is that it allows the plant to direct its entire energy towards producing more fruit, as opposed to directing part of this to growing, in order to compensate for what you have cut...

As for watering, the magic vineyard did not use modern systems at all. He explained to us that the plant has its own ancient way of dealing with draught and flooding, by adjusting its roots—expanding them when it rains and withdrawing when it's dry. Again, this is a model of energy self-management, as it reduces the effort allocated to the search of water and redirects to the grapes. Therefore, even though the harvest is smaller in terms of quantity in the years with poor rain, the quality is much better, as the fruit is sweet and aromatic, and so the wine will inherit an exquisite bouquet.

All these may seem impractical in our industrialized world, where vineyards are managed by means of standard programs, maximizing harvest and ensuring optimal times for production; and where the plants are irrigated automatically and cut at a specific height, allowing harvesting machines to fit between the lines and pick everything, observing a perfect calendar.

So yes, it might be not the most efficient wine producer in the region, but the harmony and passion that surrounded the place invaded all my senses in a wonderful way that Saturday. And I knew that small community could survive any crisis, given their love for nature and passion for work. I was breathing normality, for the first time in a long while, on the top of a hill where an Austrian relocated years before, married a Moldavian beauty and were adopted as such by the locals.

A nice and simple late lunch followed, and all thoughts melted away in a symphony of taste that transported me back to childhood—traditional Romanian appetizers and main courses that reminded me (once again!) of my grandmother's courtyard, and our family meals in the shadow of an old quince tree.

After the intense heat, an incredibly heavy rain came down in the evening, on our way back. The minibus needed to slow down close to stopping, as the road seemed to pass straight through the heart of a cascade for a while. Lightning and thunder surrounded us, while we went by two gas stations that had run out of service, due to electrical power failure. Finally we arrived back to the city, where it was again dry and hot, no rain and no wind at all. Hot night followed.

The next day I went visiting my cousins, somewhere close to the mountains—quiet and not so hot, rainy but not so heavy. I cannot remember how we got to that point, but my cousin started talking about our grandfather. I always knew he was an orphan, but I never asked my mother about details, somehow I presumed he was born without a family, as this was my understanding of "orphan" while growing up. That Sunday I learned that he crossed the war line from Russia to Romania (to the place where he would later meet my grandmother), after both his parents were killed. He came all by himself to the household of one of his aunts, and she took him in. He was a teenager at that time.

My mind strolled to my grandmother again and how she defied the rules of her time, refusing to accept an arranged marriage. She wanted a "town boy" instead of a land owner, which was available in the village (mostly vineyards in that area...), so she decided to wait until she got her dream, in the person of my grandfather. The family was quite outraged, as she was the older sister and there were priority rules back then. She also survived several nasty war experience, such as hostile soldiers chasing her down the hill; she managed to escape, but was under both physical and mental shock for a while. Yet I always remember her beautiful laughter and positive energy—never compromising on optimism, as even her favorite cursing exercises made us laugh our heads off...

Those two simple folks had four kids and lived long, healthy, happy and respected lives, obeying by a basic honorable principle: being dignifiedly poor, while affording to get whatever they reasonably wished for. All four kids were sent to school up to university, and they were always ready for helping others within the community.

My mother also had learned quickly to walk her own way. An early marriage was followed by divorce because she refused to accept an abusive husband, no matter how dramatic the implications of her decision seemed to be (including life threats from a lawyer with a gun permit...). She wanted a family and especially kids and she finally had all that—even though quite late in her life.

My mother was always opened and truthful, even though it wasn't the safest way to approach career in a communist country... She was a teacher and a mother, standing up for what she believed to be important, and thus she has educated generations of good people in the same spirit. She was generous on both spiritual and material matters and used to tell us girls that it was better to lend than to borrow, while one should be careful to whom one gives money—never lend again to whoever did not honor their previous debt. She also taught us to set aside "white money for black days" and not to expect anything back when helping someone in distress.

All those teachings look like sound principles still today.

And then there was my father. I never met his parents and he was quite an enigmatic person for me, partially because I had little time to get to know him. He was around only for the first 14 years of my life, then he passed away, probably taking care of his family from a higher level...

He was quite stubborn and did not want to join the Communist (and only) Party, even though it was required for his job (they never fired him however, as it seems he was good at what he was doing...). I remember his sense of humor but also his quick temper and his story-telling, passion for food and wines. And, of course, his poetry... everything in my father's life seemed to be as big as his heart!

And of course there were also my uncles and aunts, cousins and nephews, all with their own life story, with personal and family virtues and flaws, all of us starting from the same grandparents that were so close to getting killed in the war before meeting each other, but managed to survive and smile with hope upon the future. From this part of the family I was especially fond of one uncle, from whom I collected many lessons, including pure generosity. He used to say: never ask your guests if they want anything just lay down the table, give whatever you can share and let them choose if they want something! (Does this sound familiar when talking about banks vs. borrowers and the debate about who is more to be blamed—the one who offered or the one who took?)

I am here today coming from exceptional parents, who each went through failed marriages and surfed through tough communist times, in a wise manner, managing to create and harness a happy and self-protective family oasis.

You may wonder by now why so much of this chapter is about the story of my big and happy family. Don't worry, as I will come to the point soon.

Late evening the same Sunday mentioned above, after leaving my cousin's company, I got on the plane to return to Vienna, in order to start a new working week. After two days of intense emotions, I was meditating on those memories and felt the need to write down a piece of personal history. I closed my eyes and re-lived the deep breath taken in the same places where my parents and grandparents used to live.

And then, all of a sudden, on the way from the airport train to my apartment in Vienna, a heavy rain started. We had experienced quite a hot summer that year, with storms coming out of nowhere, without warning or estimate about how long or how nasty they could get. I looked around and saw people running for shelter, then closed my eyes and imagined my teenage grandfather crossing the enemy line during the war, looking for a new home...

I do not know if it was raining that day (or week, or month...), while he was walking and hoping for a better future. I also do not know for how long he had to run, or hide and then keep on running and hiding, until he arrived safely at his destination. I just knew that I was less than 15 minutes away from my home and, more important, that I knew exactly where that was and how to get there. Yes, it was raining and the wind was blowing and I was basically freezing after the hot weekend left behind on a distant airport just a couple of hours before. So I looked up to the sky, smiled to my grandfather and started to walk through the heavy rain. I got completely wet and took a dive straight in the bath tub when I got home, appreciating the fact that everything around was safe and familiar.

Somewhere in between the lunch table from my cousin's courtyard and that hot bath tub I understood that we perceive crisis in relation to our comfort circle, within our expectations regarding normality and correlated to our very demanding life standards.

I decided then and there that I would take a break from the "Roots" series and start looking ahead, for some ways out of what seemed to be an over-pessimistic spiral. I would be of much bigger help by seeking how to bring the morale back into our life, reasonability back into our expectations, humility and altruism into our attitude.

A dear friend told me something important some years ago. I asked him what he found most scary in life and he told me it was the thought of waking up one morning not being able to look at himself in the mirror, because of something he had done.

This is how I decided to start the "WAYS" series—by inviting everyone to think about their morning mirror.

If you like what you see there, please start tomorrow focused on maintaining or even improving that; if you don't, then do something about it, start changing your ways so that you would like yourself again soon! Do not focus too much on the other mirrors around, where people look and see either whatever you want them to see or whatever they want to see in you. Just make your own reality and morality check, ask yourself what you would do better today to get a better mirror image when you wake up tomorrow.

I believe this could be a good start. It may not solve the global crisis yet, but should at least bring a slightly different perspective on it.

WAY 2—THE LESSON

Motto:
"Always when judging
Who people are,
Remember to footnote
The words 'So far.'"

Robert Brault

My first trip to Barcelona came in the summer of 2012.

Beautiful town on the seaside, where the plane landed from... the sea side. Most of the flying also happened above the sea, making me quite nervous, as I am not a fan of deep water, even knowing that going down in the sea would be safer than crashing into some mountains. But the thought of my modest swimming know-how turned my stomach into the home of a hundred ants, so it took some time to relax and enjoy the view—exquisite otherwise.

I will not bore you with details about the holiday, but take you straight back to the return flight.

This time I was really nervous, that kind of "I-have-a-bad-feeling" nervousness. Just in front of me at the boarding was a Russian family with a little daughter, looking like one of those perfect kids you see in the commercials—a curly Blondie, with round rosy cheeks and deep blue eyes, observing everything around with curious while playful childish look. On the left of the airplane at the entrance, the door to the pilot's cabin opened and the warm voice of the captain invited the little lady to look inside, without being shy. The father was impressed and started to thank for this and the immediate effect was that the entire family was invited to look in. I started to wonder if the pilot was some terrorist who was planning to blow up the plane and this would be his last good deed before the final gesture...

We settled in, and then the plane begun to move. While we were still on the runway, the captain started to talk to us. He welcomed us on board, told us that we are flying to Vienna (good-at least I was on the right plane!) and then informed us that there was a storm ahead, so he would need to go around it. Also good, so perhaps my bad feeling is not connected to a bomb but to a storm... this should be better, as I already survived some of those.

Then the same voice invited us all to look to the left immediately after the take-off, as we would fly along the coast, to get a chance to say good-bye to the nice beaches of Barcelona. I thought to myself "ok, nice relaxing exercises" and prepared to extend my neck as far as socially acceptable without biting into my left neighbor's right ear. And then the funniest thing happened—the guy actually turned the big plane to the left so suddenly after we rose from the ground, that I thought for a second he will dip the wing into the water and we will actually shake hands with the people on the beach to say an official goodbye. And then another funny thing happened—after we did the grand tour of the beaches, he turned again... to the right! This time really heading home...

Well, now I started to wonder whether next he will tell us his wife dumped him, this is his last flight and he wanted to let us die with a nice memory of Barcelona's beach in our heads. But then, quite soon after this, the voice started to talk to us again. This time he was mentioning that we can actually see the day—night limit line on one side. He was right! Then he told us on which side we can see Nice. By that time I was already relaxed, thinking that as long as he is flying that plane nothing wrong can happen, as he obviously loves to do it. I started to feel like in a hop-on / hop-off trip, only nicer. I even wondered if we should tip the pilot on our way out.

Later on, he apologized that we could feel a little shaky, kindly asked us to buckle up and at the same time pointed out that to the left there was that big black nasty storm he told us about, with incredible lightning illuminating the clouds from within, a unique spectacle under which (unfortunately not possible to see) there was another nice town (cannot remember which). Interesting was also that I felt no real shaking compared to what I have experienced in some other cases even on clear weather...

And so, he kept on showing us amazing things out of the window until we arrived in Vienna, and the flight attendant said her routine "thank you, hope you fly Austrian again and goodbye". Then, immediately after landing, his smiling voice also added simple but warm "Thank you, I wish you good night and a nice stay in Vienna." I must say that night I saw a complete different face of Austrian pilots—even though I should not use the plural. I am sure I would not experience a similar flight any time soon.

I was not surprised at all (but almost expected) to see the cabin door opened when we left the plane, him standing with a big smile on his face in the door and saying goodbye to each of us. I did not expect him to be so young and tall, suntanned and blue eyed (or maybe not blue but nicely eyed anyway...), but I managed to close my mouth and put my eyes back in their respective eyeballs rather elegantly, probably I also shared a smile in return (even if I could not swear to that...).

I arrived home late at night, with a big smile on my face and several lessons learned.

First, that there are people that can do their "routine" job, without forgetting that for others the same sequence of events is nothing short of a miracle. And so someone can make the best of it—not only focus on delivering highest professional standards in their work, but going one step forward and bringing a human dimension, caring about the smiles on people's faces and the drops of happiness in their blood.

The second lesson was that we could very well fly through life at high speed, not looking left or right and believing that reaching the destination is enough; sure way to miss a lot of spectacular views...

Third—that sometimes we cannot see for ourselves, so there is a need for someone else to guide our eyes to the right picture.

The fourth lesson was that "detour" on take-off: the shortest way between two points and the nicest way between two points are very different things. Taking the time to see the beauty of a place (or in case of relationships of a person) enriches the life, no matter if the detour is short or long. Sometimes a nice detour may prove to be the actual way. From the detour I also learned another lesson, which was to always expect the unexpected (why on Earth did I assume that the beaches were in the direction of our way home?!). So, whenever you find yourself somewhere else than intended please regard this as a "detour" and enjoy—it usually comes in nice packages. Or at least with good lessons.

And finally the "last but not least" lesson was that hundreds of ants in the stomach can also predict something nice or can predict nothing at all. The feeling can be related to the pure fact that I might have ingested hundreds of ants over dinner.

And those were only one-afternoon lessons.

I will now take you to another place—a nice quiet restaurant in Bucharest, where I was with a dear friend of mine. She told me that the "most beautiful age" from her point of view was 43. I took it as good news, as it was still slightly ahead of me at that time (not any longer though!). A question however popped up rather quickly: why 43 and not 40 or 45 or 36? Her answer was that exactly at that age she became really comfortable with everything about herself—inside and outside.

And then I started to wonder whether I already passed the best age, as I realized it had nothing to do with the calendar. The lesson I learned that day was that the sooner one reaches the most beautiful age, the longer it might last. It could be a couple of years, a decade or even more. I started to better understand why women tend to omit mentioning their age as they grow older, and it seemed to me that they would just avoid labels and conventional judgment. Young ones might pretend to be older and vice-versa and the same might go for men also. It looked like not important anymore after reaching the beautiful age, obviously until... it would start to matter all over again.

Everything in life is cyclical and so I come to the second lesson at that table: the link between personal life and career.

She made me open my eyes to the fact that if I was to live a long life (which I do wish—and also to all of my readers!), then inherently ups and downs would cross my path. Every career brings along challenges, sometimes followed by satisfaction, other times by disappointment; sometimes one just gets good money out of it, other times status or just peace; sometimes respect, other times humiliation; sometimes power, other times endurance. The most important part is to extract at least one lesson out of each of those phases and move on. This could mean enjoying also periods of quietness, sometimes even taking some steps back to recharge batteries from the other side—the personal one.

Starting with early school years, continuing in university and later on in our professional life, we learn that in the global contemporary economy the most valuable features of a winner should be a cool head and cold heart (for thinking clearly), decorated with big eyes and even bigger ears, small mouth and educated nose, two strong feet (for stepping over others) and agile hands (for grabbing opportunities).

On the other hand, mostly undesirable (at least for managerial positions) are those character features associated with softness—compassion, empathy, trust... which sometimes accumulate physically into sensitive and oversized parts of the body, such as the chest (may be fostering a big heart...), and the behind (it is difficult to cover your a's if it is oversized...).

Setting the joke apart, above exaggerations could help one identify those ill-intended and/or incapable professionals with wicked character, in order to minimize the negative effect of the interaction with such folks. Never underestimate those people, but also do not let them spoil your day... too often!

Personally, I have to admit to being professionally blessed to work with many good people, striving to learn as much as possible from all my past bosses and experiences.

What could then be a recipe for success in one's professional life?

Putting a piece of one's heart and soul into every day work, adding passion, strong beliefs and ethical principles—all those usually make the difference between work and career. At the same time, such approach may have unexpected outcome bordering to professional self-endangerment, as it gradually creates an eye in the storm, in which others may easily push you or you can even get pulled all by yourself. In some cases you might get exposed to changes that have greater amplitude and lower predictability than the average, such as going to sleep in Kansas with a promising career and waking up next day away from Kansas and without your red shoes[26]. Therefore, if you build your whole life around Kansas dreams, all those storms may have a tribute on your health, ability to give and accept love, to forgive and forget, to accept and embrace.

Coming back to 2012 summer holiday, it actually ended with one of the greatest and at the same time saddest lessons of life.

While preparing to go to the airport on a Sunday evening, a sweet puppy got out of the safety of our courtyard and the next thing we knew we had to bury her. I got on the plane and got back to Vienna very sad, not thinking about the holiday any more, as it seemed petty compared to that life, taken away from us in just one second.

---

[26] Reference to Dorothy in The Wonderful Wizard of Oz /L. Frank Baum

However that was also one of the reasons I could not let the week pass without sharing these lessons. All that chain of events made me understand that thinking back on one's life experiences learning something out of any event, no matter how sad, could be the most important way to approach our future. And so I decided to count the number of lessons I would absorb in a day. The good news is that it is hard, as they are so many! And usually come associated with physical sensations and the memory of hits or hugs (imaginary but feeling so real!).

It would be nice if everyone could visualize and correlate its own lessons both with past memories and future plans. As such, the good experience could be applied immediately, starting the next day, while the negative one would be better processed in time, allowing the learning to absorb wisely. However, no happening should be forgotten or ignored, but revisited from time to time until properly understood, in a constructive way that would turn us into better human beings!

Recognition for being the pettiest and meanest "kid on the block" is constantly subject to competition, while for wise and kind people the world is always big enough.

When you look out your window, focus on that part of the human kind which is good and beautiful, join forces and trust that together we may overcome any crisis! Then be patient when taking care of the wounds of those who are busy fighting and competing against each other... their healing will be facilitated by the power of our example, while we exercise our capacity to be happy!

WAY 3—THE PATIENCE

Motto:

"Patience is the companion of wisdom."

St. Augustin

It is a universal truth that with every day of our lives, we are getting older.

We can of course chose any other word instead of "older", there is quite a wide range—smarter, wiser, nicer, richer, or fatter. However those would be no longer acceptable as universal truths, because we evolve differently during our timeline, depending on a great number of factors.

I was browsing through the Quote Garden[27], like every time when planning to write something, in search of a nice motto. As expected, patience is regarded mostly as a virtue, the aptitude of wise people, thus should be qualifying perfectly as one of the ways out of our contemporary crisis.

However, some argumentation behind this nomination would be needed—if only for those people who cannot wait to understand.

---

[27] http://www.quotegarden.org/index.html

The main reason that comes to mind is purely subjective, as I admire it in some people. The bad news is that it is not so easy to recognize, as not all those who do not (re)act can be qualified as patient. There is a fine line between virtue and weakness, just as in case of most character features.

What would then be a practical definition of patience in my view?

I would describe "patience" as a certain type of action (or lack of an obvious action), at a certain moment and/or sustained for a certain period of time, triggered by a certain evaluation of a certain situation, correlated with a certain decision regarding the best choice of action, with the ultimate purpose of achieving a certain goal in the wisest possible manner.

Have I lost you? Just go back slowly and read it again. It may help putting in a relevant context, from your own experience, when you consider to have been really patient.

I cannot be sure that all relevant aspects are included in the above definition, however if any of those are missing, then the attitude cannot be qualified as patience. If either timing is wrong or evaluation of the situation improper or choice of action (or lack of it) mistaken or in case the ultimate purpose is not achieved, then we actually deal with bad results or at the least with missed opportunities.

The most frequently encountered mistakes made by impatient people are either uselessness (unneeded actions which neither harm nor help anyone, being just a waste of energy) or destructiveness (taking damaging actions before understanding the situation). Telling the difference is important for the impact on the community, as some actions which seem just useless for some, may prove destructive for others.

Sometimes the actions of the impatient can be constructive, but this would be mostly triggered by coincidence. A chain of such lucky events can trigger the persistence of the impatient in his / her behavior and even a gradual worsening of the destructive potential. Usually such person is not even ill-intended, as in case of planned destructive behavior we usually deal with patient planners.

At the other end of the spectrum lies the inert, non-responding or inactive folks, as such attitude does not qualify as patience. Just waiting for too long before answering a question or endlessly gathering data before acting in a certain direction is also damaging.

The wisdom comes from knowing exactly when it is time to act and when to wait (and see or listen or gather more information). This kind of knowledge is partially inherited, partially educated and partially driven by experience. The sooner one experiences harmful effects of impatience, the faster one gets better at intervening at the right moment or choosing the right battles. Just like John Dryden said almost 400 years ago: "Beware the fury of a patient man".

Do not be fooled however—such approach is not a universal solution to avoid conflict, damage or mistake. On the contrary, patience can be also a dangerous weapon when in hands of bad characters, as it can serve as well good and evil individuals. Therefore, it is also important to understand the profile and intentions behind one's actions—there are those which mean well (either enthusiastically in a hurry or innocently indolent) and those with bad will, which pursue a planned destructive approach (no matter if they are patient or not).

As for myself, I am still learning patience, every day. The most important lesson up to now is that the best possible teacher is negative experience. Obviously, attitude does not change overnight, as a good part of human reactions are subconsciously driven by temperament. That does not mean that we should not exercise patience as frequently (and fast?!) as possible, and preferably start with "at-ease" situations, before beating our head against walls on important matters.

Cooking played a big role in self-educating my patience, and I resonate very much with Paul Sweeney[28], as he asked himself "How can a society that exists on instant mashed potatoes, packaged cake mixes, frozen dinners, and instant cameras teach patience to its young?"

My childhood was a constant lesson of culinary patience, from queuing for food to waiting until small miracles would come out of the kitchen. It always seemed too long when you manually needed to mix the eggs with the sugar, so they become puffy enough for the cake. Afterwards I was always amazed about how long half an hour can be when you are not allowed to open the oven door, no matter how curious you were (main question back then being whether the cake was really growing, as everything happened secretly behind a metal door before the age of the thermo-resistant glass!). Once you opened it prematurely, the disaster was guaranteed...

I also knew since I was three years old how long it takes to get to my grandmother by train and already learned that sleeping and talking would make the time go faster. And I was never really a

----

[28] Irish writer (b. 1955)

train sleeper... I still remember one such a trip when it stopped in the middle of nowhere, for more than two hours. It was a very hot summer and people were really upset about the situation, until I started to tell them a classic Romanian story, called Harap Alb (you know, the good guy goes after emperor's daughter, the bad guy tries to kill him, a magic horse being also involved—and all ends up well). Even my mother was fascinated of the twists and turns of my version of the story, that made it last exactly as long as the train was stuck—and it came with my first material gain, a small puppet that I kept as valuable trophy for a long time.

The point is that usually there is a direct (but reasonable!) correlation between good things and waiting time.

I was seven years old when a Romanian movie called "Hurry up slowly!" had its premiere at the cinema. My mother liked the title so much (the movie was also ok...), that she tried for years to carve those words into my mind. I believe she was never really happy with the results of her efforts, as I was always more the type "Oh God, give me Patience! NOOOOW!"

Only much later I came to learn that slowing down and taking time to understand things may be more productive sometimes, instead of just acting based on first round of information and heated emotion. It's always a matter of properly assessing the situation at hand, so there is something to be learned from stones, rivers and trees, but also from birds and bees, predators and prays. We should learn to be patient without forgetting that we need to act in time, efficiently and in the direction of our purpose.

Much closer to present times I have been travelling again a lot—by plain this time. There were not many delays; however one was particularly notable, on a Sunday night, going back to Vienna after a relaxing week-end in Bucharest with my family.

Upon arrival at the airport, the plane was already announced one hour late for take-off. The numbers rolled quickly into 1.5 hours. I could think of several certain effects of the delay, some unpleasant (arriving late, sleeping less), some pleasant (writing down something after a long pause). As for the indirect or uncertain effects, I did not waste time thinking about that, as anyhow the delay would shift everything forward and who would know what would have happened (or not) if not... you get the point!

Fellow passengers seemed mostly grumpy and unhappy with the situation—some were losing connections (trains, planes...), others would need to spend more to reach their destination (e.g. cab instead of train). The air was filled with discomfort and impatience... and in the middle of all that I was wondering what to do with all that free time. For sure it needed to be something nice, as the only method (empirically tested!) to accelerate the passage of time.

I could read, talk on the phone, socialize, write or just sit and meditate (which in my case means day-dreaming, nothing to do with any Tibetan or other kind of spiritual practice!). In front of my closed eyes popped out an advertisement which I liked—a poster on a bus, campaigning against smoking by suggesting alternatives lasting the same as a cigarette; the funniest was the "nothing" solution.

I decided to excuse myself from the circle of waiting friends, confessing that there are moments when my social personality goes to sleep and in such moments I withdraw and write. And so I was already half way through a blog posting when the phone rang—it was my niece, about four years old at that time. The miracle happened with the large support of my sister (her mother), who decided to grant her a wish—she just wanted to call somebody! And so I started a conversation with three angels, which lasted for several minutes that otherwise would have been spent boarding. As such, we exchanged pure joy and some good laughs, while they fed me exactly the needed material for my writing, even if they did not know what was happening at the other end of the wire (actually lack of wire).

My niece did not say much, just "hello and when do you come back?" My sister then told me how the little one was so terrible, never patient enough to let her mother speak, no matter whom they call... just slashes the phone out of her hands or jumps yelling all around, so nobody can speak...

Then my nephew followed (almost six years old), asking me bluntly why am I not taking the car, if the plane does not come. That was a logical and perfectly justified question, demonstrating early inclination towards solution-finding! I explained to him that it would last almost a full day to get to Vienna by car, so it would still be faster by plane, even if delayed for a couple of hours.

This made me think again about evolution of transportation means on a historical scale, and how easy we can move around the world today, in exchange for quite a modest price. With every technological step ahead, our patience is melting away, both on an individual and global scale. Despite already extraordinary accomplishments, we still want more and faster changes, while having less patience for understanding, testing, exploring, or comparing. We experiment all kind of new things (solutions, products, medicine, treatments etc.), without considering that in some cases generations need to fully develop before we could correlate consequence with root cause. We engage in a spiral of compulsive buying of expensive new technologies, before we even understand how we would benefit from them or even if we can afford them, and thus fueling the systemic crisis all around.

It seems to me that we are trapped into a paradox of own impatience—the faster we go, the longer it takes us to get anywhere, as the destination keeps on shifting ahead of us. Unfortunately the history is written in a subjective and distorted manner, which compliments only the winners, therefore we have no idea what warning signs could signal that a civilization is headed for self-destruction. That Sunday night in the airport one idea emerged inside my mind: what if, at a certain point in their evolution, the great extinct ones just... lost their patience? And, because of that, engaged in some monumental and irreversible mistakes, on a planetary scale?

It seems rather hard to imagine that a systemic snowball could be stopped on an individual level. Still, patience can be (re)instilled in each one of us, by carefully choosing our models in life, and by learning something from each lesson that crosses our path. It takes of course commitment, perseverance and... a lot of patience!

The way in which wise people choose to welcome patience into their lives is actually correlated with the second root—"The Tolerance". Such a person should know just how much can be tolerated without action, what action needs to be taken and why, when and for how long, in what direction and with which instruments, so that the result is consistent with the intended purpose.

Respective harmony is best achieved when both decision and action come naturally, part intuitive and part reasoned, in a beautiful combination of self-confidence, maturity and courage. And in order to get there, some of us may need a lifetime, some less while some... even longer than that!

WAY 4—THE MANAGER

Motto:
"Never point a finger where you never lent a hand."
Robert Brault

The idea of the "good manager" is hosted by the "Ways" series mostly because of the intent to steer towards improvement and growth, instead of blame games and resentment. Of course "The Manager" can be always re-assessed as a "Roots" chapter, by simply focusing on the negative side and acknowledging the fact that our contemporary crisis is deeply rooted, amongst other things, also into pure mismanagement—on different levels, in many areas of our life.

To put things into perspective, I would not refer only to the professional universe, as management is a part of our larger reality. Every human being administers resources and influences destinies on a daily basis, as natural as breathing, eating, or sleeping. Even assumed passiveness is just another way of living! We all act on a subconscious level most of the time, as instinctual managers of our private life, in relation to our families and social circles.

Under this perspective, a successful leader is just a regular person who integrates efficiently available resources, understands and explores with agility surrounding circumstances, estimates possible evolutions and elaborates alternative scenarios, takes firm decisions in real time and brings it all together by acting, consequently and flexibly at the same time, towards the chosen goal.

Far from being a linear process, the management activity unrolls on many parallel plans, which are integrated periodically, with certain cyclicality. Periods of growth (or regress) rely on different drivers—financial gain, market quota, customer awareness and so on. The cycles are alternated sometimes in line with internal priorities (process improvement, resource allocation, mergers or acquisitions etc.), while other times are driven externally (market, customers, macro changes etc.).

An efficient manager should be capable to fit in all relevant aspects for best results, no matter the level in the hierarchy. Harmony inside an organization cannot be reached and maintained exclusively from the top, as it is the responsibility of all its internal stakeholders. I am not a fan of excessive specialization on a managerial level, quite the contrary! Experience has led me to believe that people that have a shared understanding of their roles and complementarities, are more capable of performing as an integrated system, without gaps in (or redundancies between) the processes.

Enough introduction, let's get started!

What you are about to read may seem as an excessive simplification of the managerial function, emerging from the idea that life is beautiful when governed by minimalism. Therefore, this chapter is structured from the perspective of prioritization. As a take-away the readers should get an imaginary hand-book with practical hints about simple focus areas, in order to induce progress in their relevant communities, pulling it out of any specific crisis.

The journey starts with exploring three basic principles: the first is that there is no business ethics, but just ethics; the second is that both the way and the destination are important; and the third: every person is unique.

The first principle was introduced by John C. Maxwell[29], who believed that there was no "special" ethics for business life, just another part of the general life principles. In other words, one cannot be a liar and jerk at work and at the same time a good, flawless Christian in the privacy of own home, or vice-versa, have questionable conduct in personal life while being a role-model as an employee.

I remember one debate with a professional peer, the same year when I decided to return to Romania. He challenged this principle by saying that sometimes it proves to be difficult to apply the same standard, especially in our line of work[30]. He gave the simplest example—daily dealing with crooks (to whom we would not give the time of day otherwise!), striving for reasonable compromise in order to protect our employer's legitimate interest. He underlined that most probably in our personal life we would not be inclined towards similar amiable solutions but draw a line and choose to fix our losses and learn the hard lessons.

His question made me ponder for a while, but in the end my answer was "Yes, I do believe in this as a general principle". The ethical fundament behind such logic can be resumed in two simple

---

[29] John C. Maxwell (bestselling author, coach, and speaker on leadership topics), in his book 'There's no such thing as "Business Ethics"'

[30] bad loans management

words: "No more!" Most human beings divide the world around in good and evil, black vs. white extremes, with myriad of shades of grey in between. I visualize the individual ethical code as an imaginary red line that cuts through the grey zone, by connecting the dots we use for discerning between right and wrong. The exact points where the line crosses in a certain context and at a certain moment of one's life varies under the influence of many elements—education, religion, experience, people and relationships involved, specifics of the situation etc.

The theory of small steps tells us that the red line is dynamic—gradually sliding either towards the darker side of the spectrum (when exposed to negative experience, slowly increasing in frequency and intensity), or towards the brighter side (as positive experience raises our expectation for the best). Everything revolves around individual tolerance level (see also Root 2—The Tolerance).

As we grow older, we are on the one hand spoiled by nice surprises and accomplishments, on the other hand frustrated by hardship and injustice. Therefore, we become either more generous or opened, or just the opposite—less tolerant and suspicious of others. Dilemmas in our personal and professional lives are clearly different; however we still approach with the same red line, by shifting it accordingly one way or another. And the personal comfort with our decisions is being checked at least on a daily basis, in the mirror.

Moving now to the second principle, I consider ways and destinations to be equally important, based on a similar logic to the "hen and egg" dilemma.

To cut this short, no manager can start a journey without setting a goal. Despite the fact that the way seems usually the best part of the experience, the future success is defined only in combination with achieved results—fulfillment or frustration, glory or disgrace.

The third principle is self-explanatory, as people are also known as "individuals"—unique and inseparable from themselves. It is therefore highly productive not to develop parallel personalities at home and at work, so that we can act naturally and have a reasonable satisfaction level, as complete persons. Another aspect of our uniqueness is that even if some leadership abilities may be improved by adult education, most of them are either genetically encoded or built into our character at an early age, therefore they manifest intuitively most of the time.

Last but not least, on an individual level, personal priorities should be harmonized with professional ones, so that no conflict arises between them. While this is obviously no easy task, it is an essential feature for reaching a sustainable balance and overcome any type of stress.

All those being said, let's start the outlines for the practical handbook, aimed to identity focus areas one should address for leading a successful life during difficult times.

The first thing to look at would actually be... the results! Most part of the efforts should be focused on this, as the basic idea of "managing" relates to a destination. One can of course wonder around and do beautiful things out of luck and without any direction, but that definitely cannot be considered management.

So, before we start leading others, we need a purpose, an idea of what we aim to accomplish. The definition of expected result is called target or objective and it may change along the journey.

One of the most important (and beautiful) aspects of successful management is exactly the dynamism of the scope. In normal environments, everyone deals concomitantly with more than one objective and there is always a relationship between various results. Sometimes this is clear and can be anticipated, other times it is hidden and therefore unforeseeable. A good manager recognizes if and when the direction needs adjustment and stops before going down on an unrealistic road and thus damaging a bigger picture which is being pursued.

Let's take an example: flying from point A to point B. The simple mathematical way to optimize this route is to fly on a straight line—fast and efficient. However if we add restrictions such as no-fly zones or adverse weather conditions, it might happen that the plane would need to take an alternative route, which may seem irrational for someone who is unaware of the real situation. Furthermore, on a long haul trip to exotic destinations, unless direct charter is available, one may need to change 2 or 3 planes to get there. Ultimately, while the plane is in the air, a number of technical malfunctions might force the pilot into an emergency landing decision in order to ensure safety, therefore deliver the passengers to a point C that was not part of the initial planning.

Obviously the outcome varies both in terms of quantity and especially quality, therefore one of the biggest challenges of management is to describe as reasonably as possible what is expected. You may remember the "Cast Away" movie with Tom Hanks—the parcel gets delivered in the end; whether that is an acceptable result or not, depends of course on the way you look at it...

The objective is something the manager targets to achieve and it has to do with the future. Does it also have to do with the actual act of management? Yes and no. Yes, as it is the crucial element shaping the day-to-day actions. No, as if we want to make God laugh we just need to show Him our plans... Confusing... what would then be a manager expected to do? The simplest answer is: to manage his/her team's way towards the best result. How?

Let's look now at the potential points of intervention, one by one.

First of all, a good manager puts all available resources to the best possible combined use.

What does "available" mean? Not only whatever one already has, but also what can be reasonably obtained in order to accomplish the objective. How limited are those resources? It depends on the category of the resource but also on the creativity and personality of the manager and the team. A golden rule about resources is that there is a right place, time and purpose for everyone and everything. Sometimes special situations may appear, which can be tackled with exceptional approach, however in the long run one must clearly understand the structure, strengths and weaknesses of own resources in order to use them sustainably and efficiently.

In an over-simplified manner, resources may be grouped in material ones (anything from buildings and equipment, to simple paper and vital coffee), financial, information and intellectual property, time and human factor (not only staff or family, but also the social network indirectly linked to them).

In my experience, human capital is the most important resource for the success of any personal or professional enterprise, the only one who can actually give a purpose to all the rest and have a decisive influence in the quality of the result. The same amount of information processed with comparable material means over a similar period of time, by different people, will translate into various knowledge patterns and generate diverse interpretation and correlation paths, thus delivering dissimilar results.

The second aspect on which a good manager needs to focus is management of circumstances.

On daily basis, things tend to happen all around. Few situations are really neutral on the participants, most of them represent either opportunities or threats for the future chain of events and the humans involved in them. Those effects are commonly referred as consequences. What is also interesting is the fact that every person notices different things from a similar event (that is if anything is noticed at all!). Therefore, one needs to be as attentive as possible to everything that happens all around and at the same time as assertive as possible, interpreting and correlating potential consequences which may arise, then translate most of them into opportunities. A crucial part of the result delivery is exactly personal understanding of the situations, weighting them against each other, aligning to strategic goals and available resources (or vice-versa!). In this process, a good manager should be ready even to adjust expectations if it proves to facilitate an overall improvement of the outcome.

Time is an essential factor when dealing with situations—there is no use to implement a perfect plan if the intervention comes too late. Proper priority setting, quick decision-making and the ability to mobilize (and motivate!) resources even before having all the details actually make the difference between game changers, survivors and the ones left behind. The decisive parameters in the equation of success are experience, courage and wisdom, as they allow the leader to discern when to act, based on available information, in the direction of the strategic goal. On the other hand, ignoring relevant details or underestimating circumstances may prove to be fatal, and so would be allocating resource for pursuing unachievable objectives or useless aspirations. Darwin said it best with his "survival of the fittest" theory...

And thus, we reach the third (crucial!) focus pillar: expectations. Mature managers build them with clarity, downwards and upwards, addressing most important aspects—results and priorities, risk appetite and ethical behavior and so on. Their communication pattern is tailored for each recipient and correlated with all the other pillars.

What does this mean? As team leaders largely depend on others for delivery, there must be a fair mutual understanding for any task, when cascading down or re-distributing among peers (in terms of resource, situation and power balance), so everyone involved may assume realistic outcome (in terms of quantity, quality and timeliness).

If we take the example of a team member with a sick kid at home—one should not expect late-night work on urgent reports that can be delivered by another member or can wait for another day. If however it is a special no-way-out situation, the effort should be compensated accordingly and not repeated often, as it will damage the resource, at least in terms of enthusiasm and commitment.

Motivation is an essential part of the journey towards reasonable expectation setting. Obviously the financial component is a key driver and must be considered at all times, however it is not a stand-alone factor and must be sustained at all times with non-financial stimuli, such as recognition of professional status, respect for morals, privacy and personal balance, support for self-development, reputation.

Last but not least, as it integrates all the other focus pillars, comes the intervention tool-kit, actually the personal touch given by the personality of the manager. Millions of pages have been already written about management styles and individual typologies, while this is out of the scope of today's exercise. Instead, I would invite you to design your own favorite managerial profile and will start with an indicative list that includes enthusiasm, knowledge sharing, prioritization, motivation, delegation and empowerment (always together!), fairness and ethics, continuous learning, practical problem solving, efficiency.

Bringing all this to a conclusion, I would say that human factor and time constraint are amongst the most important focus area for a successful manager. The rest are easier to attract and put to good use, once you get those two right—everything comes to life under the direction of a leader that knows how to approach expectations around, but also from within!

At the end of the day, the secret is to enjoy the way to your goal and master resources with enthusiasm and fairness. Whenever management is perceived as a struggle, even if sometimes brings results, it's only on a short term, and definitely not viable. Life may put us in front of such situations every now and then, testing our abilities. We should be able to face such challenges as they come, and temporarily be ready to apply different tools than our usual "kit". But we should also be strong enough to come back to a more sustainable way of managing situations, to that natural style which fits best our personality and life beliefs and allows us to look to ourselves in the mirror with a smile before we go to bed. It is good both to confront our limits and re-discover our strengths periodically.

Fairness and appreciation for the people, completed by deep understanding of resources and situations, for the benefit of the result—all that sustains reputation in the long run, if we wish to overcome difficulties, be it in our daily personal life or at work.

Remember that "There is often less danger in the things we fear than in the things we desire" (John Churton Collins[31]). Be careful how you set goals and do not allow them to corrupt your ways... or the other way around!

[31] British literary critic (1848–1908)

WAY 5—THE WAY HOME

Motto:
"All men should strive to learn before they die, what they are running from, and to, and why."

James Thurber

More than twelve years ago I came across a book called "The Alchemist", by Paolo Coelho. I still remember sharing the hero's excitement about taking life into his own hands, in search for something important. I went to sleep with a smile on my face, as a feeling of comfort invaded my soul when he actually found his peace in the very place he had left in search of adventure—the original home.

There is however one question coming back from time to time: would that hero have recognized the happiness in his own home, if he wouldn't have left for a while, embarking in a travel around the world? I would say not. I believe that he needed to seek answers and calm down his restlessness before finding peace.

More recently, Robert Brault said in one of his daily wise thoughts: "Sometimes we don't find the thing that will make us happy because we can't give up the thing that was supposed to."

I liked it so much that I immediately shared it with my close friends. One of the receivers responded by raising several questions, such as "Why do we think people should be happy at all?" and "Isn't the need for happiness somehow over-stated?"

It was not the first time when I was confronted with rather similar questions, which I tend to consider rhetorical (as those people do not actually expect an answer ...). I have come in contact with such dilemmas several times over the past years, coming from separate cultures and triggered by different contexts.

One person was purely wondering if we deserve to be happy in general. He seemed to feel that because of our imperfections, flaws, bad thoughts or purely lack of focus in the pursuit of happiness, we should be realistic and not expect that someone just surrenders to us (you know... to have and to hold... with or without proper documentation these days).

The other was more inclined to say that some people are just unable to be happy, no matter how hard others strive to make them happy. They are "programmed" in such a manner that they are permanently dissatisfied with the world around them, or suspicious about people's intentions or at least this is how they perceive life evolving in the world they live in.

Finally, a more complex but rather similar question popped up in connection to one of the youngest and dearest members of my family. The question was whether a kid should learn from a very young age how to act, with intent to correct his unhappiness. Whether he should strive to change things, make them different, so that he becomes happy with the results (or at least "happier", by comparison with the initial state)?

As all life's great dilemmas, also this one should be answered under consideration of reasonable balance: yes, people should strive to change whatever makes them unhappy, they should address the pain and the hardship with the aim to improve their own situation. However at the same time one should be careful how far to go in the pursuit of own well-being, while taking care not to hurt others, assuming responsibility and not giving up on certain things to soon, just because they may bring along unhappiness for a while. Our children should learn how to set ambitious yet achievable goals, learn to differentiate as early as possible between things they can and things they cannot change, when to act and when to accept.

I have recently learned from Rebecca Saxe[32] that human abilities for issuing moral judgment regarding other people's actions and feelings are based into a certain area of our brains, which is gradually forming while we are young, from childhood throughout as far as our teenage period. Therefore children's ability to correlate happiness with moral criteria about how their actions affect others does not have to do only with education. It is also linked to the physical development of their brain, which needs to reach a certain maturity before being able to issue sound moral judgment. Until then, children are basically counting on the adult environment for support in discerning between right and wrong. Adults would better behave credibly and trustworthy when interacting with the young generation, as they are supposed to guide them through a period of both high vulnerability and curious exploration.

---

[32] American Professor of Neuro-Cognitive Science at M.I.T. (see also https://www.ted.com/talks/rebecca_saxe_how_brains_make_moral_judgments)

This being said, I wish parents good luck and a lot of patience while answering (sometimes funny!) kids' moral dilemmas! Those steps are really important while preparing for happy fulfilling lives.

And so... I started to wonder again how come that some people grow up with so different expectation and even perception about happiness. It is common knowledge that infancy sets the frame for physical and emotional readiness for life, happiness and empathy, integrity and success. It is also natural that the experience we accumulate during the adult life is the one that continuously shapes our human behavior.

I would therefore venture to say that character is formed in childhood, while wisdom is gained (if it comes at all!) throughout the entire life. Intelligence? It has to do with many influences, starting with genetic endowment, then access to education and finally also with developed personality (as curiosity and intelligence are somehow similar to the egg-hen dilemma).

You may wonder by now what all this has to do with the idea of "home", I feel compelled to get back to the topic and say... kind-of everything!

There is a common saying that home is where one's heart is. I could add a large number of other suggestions about what "home" should ideally represent. One hint that you are home is when you feel happy and serene, comfortable and safe. In that place you can share your sorrows and find courage to confront your inner demons. You can re-charge your batteries and mend your wounds. You can dream happy dreams and start building your way towards achieving those dreams. You can have nightmares and wake up knowing they will go away. Home is where you can create special rules and games for shared living, happily mixing the right proportion of freedom and dependency which define that small (or big) circle called family.

There are many individuals in our world today that are living mostly driven by adrenaline rush—no matter from where they draw it (career focus, dependencies of different sorts, Moneyteism, power fights, intrigues and gossiping, fierce competition, episodic love and so on). Wasting time, money, energy and innocence may seem painless and easy when you are young, as it still seems that all those are inexhaustible. They are not. And every individual needs to find his way home while still young enough to dream. Then start building the comfort associated with that chosen home, in order to prepare for the next phase of life—the one where the resources become obviously limited.

Sometimes I wonder why I am so innocently determined to be happy and even more, inclined to see myself as being already so. Just because... a myriad of things happen all around, making me grateful to witness their occurrence (small or big, it doesn't really matter!). Finally, I wonder why I am so committed to try everything in my power to make other people happy (or at least convince them that being happy may be good for them in the long run...).

One thing that came to my attention over the last decade was that geography has become less relevant for the perception of home, in our contemporary word. Humankind is now more dynamic than ever and the idea of contemporary home has to do mostly with non-material elements that can keep a family together.

Once we find our way home, we can also accept that we can be comfortably happy, for as long as we are. And then some...

WAY 6—THE TEACHER

Motto:
"In theory, theory and practice are the same.
In practice, they are not."

(Attributed to) Albert Einstein

Twenty-five years ago, on a nice October day, I stepped into the big festivity room of the Academy of Economic Science in Bucharest, for the official opening of my first university year. I was a fresh(wo)man. After the officials opening words of the hosts, Professor Doctor Anghel Rugină was introduced to the audience, as a prominent American Economist of Romanian origin. He was 79-years-young back then (he died in 2008, at the age of 95).

It was my first time hearing about this guy, but after a very short speech, I knew his simple words would stay with me for the rest of my life. He encouraged us, young students, to value every moment of the university years ahead and to pay attention to all our teachers, no matter how we judge them—good or bad, strong or weak, fascinating or boring, charming or not so much... and to always remember one thing: that there was much to learn also from the bad teachers, namely how NOT to behave in life, who we should prevent ourselves from becoming before being too late to straighten our ways. And that at the end of the day such corrective learning might as well prove more valuable than any positive lesson. Last but not least, he pointed out the importance of practical things that we could learn, as we should test-challenge everything while not just relying on empty theories.

As such, one autumn morning back in 1992 an eminent teacher offered to anybody who would care to listen one of the most important lessons, and he was not even on the curricula. He just came to share with a handful of young promising people some of the things he learned in life and he did that with great humility. Many lessons followed afterwards, which in the absence of this starting point would have gone by unnoticed or, even worse, inadequately absorbed by a confused adolescent, with resentment and fury instead of wisdom and focus on personal growth.

Many years after, I discovered that one of the most powerful methods of brainstorming was actually encouragement of negative thinking, especially useful when participants hit a dead end in terms of solutions and are challenged to think about making the situation worse... Negative creativity is far more imaginative while in the end some of the ideas, reversed wisely, have real potential of becoming constructive solutions.

My dear friend Peter Gluck, is another fervent supporter of the constructive power of the word "NO", and he developed a sensational set of rules for practical problem solving, in a Murphy-like negative-optimistic approach.

Another memorable day was when I realized that the Golden Rule[33], profoundly instilled in my veins since childhood, would

---

[33] Treating others as one would like to be treated him/herself.

be better applied in its "Platinum" version. More exactly, one should treat others as those would like to be treated—meaning first observe, then empathize and only then actually deliver.

And there are many more examples of past lessons, but would be totally unfair to mention some teachers while omit others. Better not mention any at all! Enough to say that I was extremely lucky, being given the opportunity to learn from everyone and everything around—family and school, work place and nature, friends and foes, dreams and reality alike.

So, why would I consider "The Teacher" as one of the focus points, in our way ahead?

No extensive arguments should be needed, as obviously our contemporary "condition" has to do with the moral hazard that gradually contaminated humanity.

The dilemmas are deeply rooted in our human nature, while purely splitting the world into 99% vs. 1%[34] will certainly not solve anything. There is no poor and pure vs. rich and rotten, just normal people giving in to daily temptation, corruption and sin. The main disparity between the 99% and the 1% lies in the type of craving they deal with—more or less expensive... otherwise, mankind is full of sinners and saints, liars and truth-holders, with reasonable distribution across regions, religions, professions and income levels.

---

[34] 'We are the 99%' is a political slogan widely used and coined by the Occupy movement (...) launched in late August 2011 (...) A related statistic, the 1%, refers to the top 1% wealthiest people in society that have a disproportionate share of capital, political influence, and the means of production (source: https://en.wikipedia.org/).

Another notable difference, conferring credibility to that split proclaimed in the 2011 global protests, is that "the 1%" have privileged access to local and global resources on the one hand, as well as control over the rules of the game and corrective actions on the other hand. They are the system lords and abuse this position basically as they please.

This being said, one should just wake up and see the reality for what it is, before hitting the self-destruct switch—meaning that... it was always like this!

Any social system, no matter how small, has its leaders—from the alpha male in the wolf-pack to the cranes that rotate as heads of the covey. Those are born and raised from within, represent the core values of the community and they all deserve each other. Sometimes, when the harmony between the chief and its flock dissipates, a brief period of instability appears, supremacy is challenged, then disputed and the fittest takes over. At the end of the day, the community gets on with its life under a new ruler—as capable, strong and respected as recognized by its own pack!

Coming back to human macro-environment, it needs this distinction, as well as the social disparities that go along with it, to make everything fall into place. Just as Pareto[35] discovered the 80/20 efficiency principle by monitoring pees in his garden, the world has recently unveiled its 99/1 power and wealth distribution by protesting in the street... but there were always kings and servants, nobles and peasants, generals and troopers, priests and sinners.

---

[35] Vilfredo Pareto (1848–1923) was an Italian engineer, sociologist, economist, political scientist, and philosopher; he stated the 80/20 rule, also known as the Pareto principle (see more on https://en.wikipedia.org/wiki/Pareto_efficiency)

The middle class, that thin layer of successful but modest people within the 99 %, has proven to be the crucial provider of high-end services, the cultural hub and the gate-keeper of morality and wisdom within the society. Historically, it included the past equivalent of contemporary entrepreneurs, those manufacturers and service providers whose prosperity was given by their ability to respond to market demand in terms of quantity, quality and timeliness. They had access to education and got the best out of the relationship with whoever could afford what they created.

And finally, there were always taxes and duties, deeply plugged into the veins of this prosperous middle class, as the only known source for long-term survival. Such levies were easier to bear in times of peace, and overwhelming in times of war. Constructions and infrastructure were flourishing during quiet periods, destroyed during conflict, and then re-built after reconciliation—and so, the wheel kept on turning. Endless growth and prosperity without sacrifice is just a fairy tale, and the 99% would better stop expecting to live in a dream world.

One question remains: if it was always like that, what did trigger the current imbalance?

How about the acute interdependence between sovereign states and the financial world? More specifically, the ruthless pursuit of voters at all costs, as they hold the key to the legitimacy of the rulers. Both sides (the 99% and the 1%) are now hostage to each other, manipulating and seeking benefits, without asking themselves who will actually pay the bill in the end. And the numbers are growing, with each new election cycle.

In theory, democracy is built on two pillars—free choice and separation of powers.

In practice, a society can only survive under condition of prosperity and peace, in a stable and functional macro-economic environment. Everything is interconnected and fueled by one circulatory structure, which is the financial system—the blood that irrigates the economy but also the State body in our contemporary world.

Also, we have to bear in mind that no humanly operated system is immune to moral hazard. And so, most of the players started to bend moral rules (at a slower or steeper pace), in order to get what they targeted—some wanted power, other wanted profit, most of them wanted both!

Do you remember the Golden Fish (you know... the one who can make dreams come true!)? How about Aladdin's lamp? Don't you feel that in the past decades, the financial system assumed this fairy-tale role for whoever wanted to make a wish come true? Car, house, political or legal power, and so on... smaller or bigger dreams. And yes, some things cannot be bought... but for everything else there is XXXX (no need to mention the credit card provider, you get the point!).

Yes, we have nice theoretical separation of powers, nice theoretically functional macro economy and nice theoretically supervised financial markets. Practically, informal systems were born out of the interaction of the theoretical ones, started to grow and lead a life of their own, just like tumors in an apparently healthy body. The doctors only noticed when it was too late and already metastatic!

As of today, it would be hard to tell which system has sinned more and who is to blame for what. All structures are practically as good as their human operators, just as it in case of regular machines or companies—their live cycle mirroring the quality of the people behind.

And thus I finally get to the point of this chapter: why do we need to redefine our Teachers?

Because we cannot kill our systems before we create something better to replace them! It would be like a mass suicide, as they are actually our working places, our sources of income, our future education and health service. We need to re-adapt them to a practically functional reality, in a way which is acceptable to our economic, cultural and moral standards.

Most communities complain that educational systems are failing—all over the world! Unfortunately, people seem to refer purely to organized school, college and university education.

I would dare to go one step further and extend this to what Peter Glück calls the new contemporary religion—Moneyteism. Let's challenge today specifically one of the new Gods—the Career God, as it is killing most of our teachers!

Career God demands many sacrifices, starting with parents who are too tired to play, friends who postpone sharing valuable experience and elders who waste precious wisdom in endless nights of loneliness. Extended family universe is dying because of lack of focus on quality personal time, while home education is crucial for a successful school impact.

Another side effect is the toxic manager, that kind of boss that sacrifices the team on the altar of own insecurity and low self-esteem. Such characters do not follow a teaching path because of misperceived competition, are always concerned about preserving their own power and thus avoid knowledge sharing at all costs.

They fear people may learn too fast and shine too much when (alas!) they should know that pupils reflect own success upon their teachers. By suffocating initiative within a team, toxic managers are basically getting in the way of their own future development.

Teacher-managers on the other hand are the ones who can spot talents and encourage them to learn as much as possible, regard them not as threats but as opportunities. The growth pool that forms around them can either provide successor ship (setting the manager free to pursue further position) or accede to peer roles within organization and expand know-how network for former colleagues. A manager who treats people as potential future stars is on the way to own personal growth.

Long-term success is therefore also an outcome of our perception about the Career God—we can see him as kind and generous or as a dangerous and vindictive creature. If we allow it to take control of our dreams, the dark side would most likely subdue us. If we can maintain balance, protect the quality of personal life while delivering high standard in our profession, we may embrace it as a Teacher. And the same goes for other Moneyteistic Gods—treating them as facilitators and learning good things from them should pave the way to a prosperous and fulfilling future.

Sometimes life seems like a marathon, spiced up by a succession of sprints. We run around, in a continuous race against time—between home, school and workplace, alongside family, friends and fellow workmates, squeezing in a drop of personal hobbies along the way (if we are lucky!). The itinerary is sometimes smooth but mostly difficult, and takes us across mountains or valleys, rivers or lakes, from quiet villages to crowded metropoles. We need as many teachers as obstacles along the way, so we can find the right balance and keep on going... and so I wonder: WHO could be that "Universal Teacher" of our next step and further ahead—our next generation?

The simplest intuitive answer that instilled in my soul is: me, you, and us—together!

We are on the one hand eternal pupils, all our lives—because we need to walk before we can run, learn before we can teach, and be proud to have lived before we can die in peace.

On the other hand, we are the teachers in our extended families, at our work place, for our friends and foes—equally. We teach by means of language, feeling and self-example, by what we do and mostly through who we are—sometimes good, other times bad, in one and the same body, materially and spiritually. Those around may learn from different angles, how they should or should not be—every day! At times they might get things wrong, misunderstand our ways and misjudge our actions... still, we should never give up being ourselves, with the permanent knowledge that we are the masters of our life and the teachers of our fellow people.

We are no saints and nobody could expect that from any of us! We are merely humans and should embrace our nature without fear or self-resentment. And as such, live our life so we can smile upon ourselves in the mirror, while remembering all the time that... WE ARE THE TEACHERS!

WAY 7—THE GIVE-AND-TAKER

Motto:
"The only people with whom you should try to get even are those who have helped you."

John E. Southard

This chapter was written on the last day of the year 2013, a year of great changes for me. It was after the summer of my coming back to Romania, while I was still not ready for saying a more permanent goodbye to my temporary adoptive country, Austria. Therefore, I kept the tradition of the previous three years and decided to spend Christmas at home with the family and for the New Year Eve I went back to Vienna.

Austrians call the last day of a year Silvester. It makes me think of the funny cat chasing Tweety in a Looney Tunes cartoon, even though the spelling is different (Sylvester). All in all, it always puts a smile on my face, encouraged also by the nice atmosphere that invades the city in this period, contributing to an optimistic disposition before the New Year Party.

For celebrating the night between the years, I have a personal check-list, which cannot be cheated: a little trip down the memory lane (what did the "old" year bring, always compared to what I wished for in the end of the previous year), a little peek into the future (what would I kindly ask from the "new" year), food and drinks in the stomach and on the table, some money in my pocket, funny outfits (especially on and around the head...), lots of noise and lots of hugging, kissing and hoping.

That day I spent the morning enjoying a late breakfast in a wonderful French restaurant called Beaulieu, in the Ferstel Passage, focusing on the memories. After that I strolled a little through the old town, and then went home to dive into a hot bubble bath, thus coming back to enjoying the present. Finally, I decided to venture with the traditional glimpse into the future, before getting out and loosing myself into the next present, once again (you know, the part with excessive eating, drinking and fire-working into the New Year).

And so I started to write, on the same familiar red couch that is actually the second biggest single contributor to what you are reading today.

I cannot remember exactly when I started to make New Year's wish lists; probably more than ten years ago... while it is not the best example of my planning abilities, they make me see how the passing of time has a way of putting things into perspective, whenever people look back on their own wishes. I always smile tenderly, remembering the "old me" who created that content.

Time has a way of sorting through what is important and lasting as compared to short day-dreaming, and usually reveals what is good for one and what is just meant to become lesson-learning.

While enjoying a hot chocolate cup that morning, I was looking around at the crowd strolling up and down the Ferstel Passage. Some people were working. There were two artists, playing a small piano and respectively a violin, filling the air with exquisite music of various backgrounds—from Viennese classics to Elvis ballads. A few waiters were bringing food and drinks, running around in perfect harmony with the surrounding music, almost as they were setting each other's pace. All of them were graciously doing their job, on the last day of the year, in exchange for a few euro and applause from us, the holiday guys and girls. We were giving them money and admiration in exchange for nurturing and beautiful future memories.

Everyone was giving and taking, in a nice set-up and with a smile on the face.

Why is this so important?

Because it may prove to be one of the easiest ways out from the contemporary self-induced and self-perceived "Crisis Ages". As pointed out in the previous chapter, our future has the face of our children. If we raise takers, we shall provide tyrants and feed abuse, intolerance and inequity in our world. If we raise givers, we shall provide martyrs and feed more abuse, intolerance and inequity... If we raise give-and-takers, we shall provide leaders and people striving on generosity and freedom of choice, thus feeding love, tolerance and prosperity in our world.

For all religions, races and cultural backgrounds, the past has proven over and over again that the only way out of any crisis created by inequity was to bring people back together, after they have hit the bottom of despair. Only by starting to give to and take from each other in an equitable manner they would find a common ground for peace and understanding. And the reciprocity I have in mind does not relate only to the material side of life, but also to housing and hospitality, moral support, love and trust and other spiritual nurturing.

Life is a multi-option, multi-choice and multi-people game, which should find its own balance once individuals accept that happiness comes from within. The give-and-take mood has more to do with feeling, perception and expectation towards society and fellowmen than with commonly measurable things. Everybody has an inherent capacity to choose and willingness to distinguish between rights and duties, carelessness and compassion, vanity and respect, manipulation and influence, hate and love, cowardice and honor and so on.

Material means are needed to achieve spiritual aspirations, and not the other way around. People should regard taking as a way to improve their giving capacity and not as a useless accumulation for own benefit. By taking love, trust or knowledge from others, one will enrich him/herself; by further sharing all those, one might enrich an entire community.

As soon as we learn to cultivate our spiritual richness and look upon life expecting the best from everyone and everything, the material world will also find a way to converge to our needs, and those two realities would just fuel each other continuously, with generosity.

WAY 8—THE DREAMER

One year passed before writing a new chapter and this time my Sylvester caught a nasty cold. He still insisted to go out in the street, therefore inhaled a lot of smoke from the fireworks, got a little fuzzy after the traditional glass(es?) of champagne and then hit the red couch and hibernated until January 2, 2015. Then my yearly lucid personality decided to come back, knock Sylvester out of my head for the next 12 months or so and started to write.

It was still middle of the yearly season for balancing past achievement with future plans, old learning with fresh expectation, and memories with dreams. During such period, I always find myself thinking about time and its effects on the perception of live, and that made me re-visit a short but interesting video[36] that treats the time perspective in a unique manner.

---

[36] RSA ANIMATE: The Secret Powers of Time (https://www.thersa.org

A large smile invaded my face, as I was absorbing several ideas and noticing details that I almost forgot were there. The same happens with the poem "Desiderata", no matter how many times I go back to it (and it happens whenever big changes are approaching). The fact is that places, songs, movies or people that I love are never boring, no matter how many times and for how long I interact with them. More than that, with every re-encounter it seems that something new comes out, fascinating and surprising, and it feels like it was not there the previous time I looked... very dear in a familiar way but at the same time mysteriously provocative.

Most people believe that happiness is about living every moment to its fullest. It might be as well true, as it is actually the only timeline in which we experience reality. The past is usually distorted by perception and the future rather unpredictable. Hence all the popular axioms, such as "seize the day", "let go of the past" and "embrace the future".

That day on the red couch, the good old Master Time revealed himself from a different perspective. It suddenly occurred to me that He was the most reliable lifetime partner we have. He is always around, not going anywhere until we take our last breath on this Earth. He clearly has split personalities (past, present and future), shifting moods (boring or exciting, predictable or fascinating, good or bad), and destiny-harmonizing skills (right or wrong), with variable driving speeds (flying by or juuuust staaaalling...).

Master Time is largely unpredictable; however in a manner that (have you noticed?) is strangely harmonized with our own impulsiveness. While I mostly agree to the general idea of living each day as it comes, (reasonably) letting go of the past and not worrying (too much) about the future, it happens that every year, on and around New Year, a little miracle affects my relationship with Master Time. His "now" personality just disappears for a little while! For several days around the New Year, he only shows his past and future selves. It is a time to reminisce and accept, then dream and foster new hopes for the future.

There is however one other little miracle that combines the various personalities of Master Time into a strange and miraculous blend between past, present and future. It does not come to us only once a year and it is called... the DREAM!

Have you ever noticed how our dreams tend to be timeless? How people from our past are sitting next to the ones from the present (even if they actually never met!) or how the future seems to be already happening as we dream? Sometimes we wake up with a slight confusion whether what we were dreaming actually happened, and it takes a little while to re-adjust. Other dreams come with no faces, no color and no time, but just a bundle of feelings. If we pay attention to those sensations, we may wake up knowing exactly what and who was that all about, even if it had no apparent content.

There are many proverbs and old sayings that try to explain dreams and what they are supposed to mean—starting with things that were forgotten and should not have been, answers to questions that we would not dare (or know how) to ask, warnings coming from the future or cries for help from our past or present. What is obvious to everyone is that they have a strong hold on our daily live, no matter whether they bring nice visions or nightmares. They each have their own distinctive contribution to reality.

Nice dreams may feel as a reward or recognition for our peace of mind, kindness and happiness, while nightmares come as warning signs, to make us more attentive to whatever is wrong. The latest may address our fears and convince us to change our mind-set or even our life for the better, in the pursuit of happiness.

Dreaming seems to be the best yet unexplained soul monitoring tool given to us by the Universe, a fine reward scheme complementing our day-to-day living. The Talmud says that "A dream which is not interpreted is like a letter which is not read."

There is some truth in this, as many visions have day-life translations. On the other hand, I do not trust universal translation rules (even though some may have empirical experience behind...), but am more inclined to believe that each reverie is tailor-made for a dialogue with ourselves and with those intimately connected to us beyond reason. As we are both creator and beneficiary of our dreams, we are obviously the main piece of the puzzle in interpreting it. As such, we should probably go beyond simple viewing towards focusing on the feelings we experience, trying to "read" between the lines whatever our subconscious mind is telling us.

There is another type of beautiful dream that has nothing to do with sleeping, just as there are actually many people in this world who believe they never dream while asleep. And I would never exclude them from pursuing one of the most beautiful ways out of the contemporary crises. That's why today's dream exploring adventure would not be complete without exploring also the so-called "day-dreams"—those great hopes for the future that we have with our eyes wide open and our minds very much awake.

We cannot call them plans, as there is a big difference, which has to do with the feasibility of the day-dream. In other words, what we wish to achieve but are not quite sure if or how or when we will, we call "dream". What is obviously within our reach, we would better call "plan".

The big challenge ahead, for strengthening our capacity to build a better future for ourselves is to rely more on our ability to dream, to properly read our dreams so we can translate them more often and faster into plans. And to further make those plans come true, in a manner that would feed better and more beautiful visions for happier and healthier future!

People should exercise more often to become skillful and beautiful DREAMERS, no matter if fantasizing while asleep, half asleep or fully awake. Then enjoy the experience of giving life to their aspirations, as a way out of any personal of global crisis—even if sometimes sacrifice would need to be made in order to get our dreams come true, for sure the satisfaction would be far more rewarding!

WAY 9—THE DANCER

Motto:
"Everything in the universe has rhythm. Everything dances."

Maya Angelou

"Dance is the hidden language of the soul."

Martha Graham

(Two independent quotes, invited to dance together by my hand today...)

Ginger Rogers, Fred Astaire, Gene Kelly, Martha Graham, Maya Plisetskaya, Rudolf Nureev, Olivia Newton-John, John Travolta, Ekaterina Gordeeva, Sergey Grinkov, Jennifer Grey, Patrick Swayze, Madonna, Michael Jackson, Shakira, Carmen Amaya, Joaquin Cortes, Michael Flattley... and the list can go on, as there are so many beautiful artists, bringing joy in our hearts and smiles on our faces, teaching us to dream about flying on a perfect music, only barely touching the dance floors.

On a quiet Sunday morning back in May 2015, as I was surfing the internet, a couple of sad news caught my attention, about the death of Ben. E. King[37] and Maya Plisetskaya[38]. Many other bad stories were popping their ugly headings on the screen, mostly reminding me that what we used to call "crisis" just a few years ago is now merely a continuous current state of affairs, no matter where we live in this world.

That Sunday however some positive news got also attention, as a new baby-princess was born in the British Royal family the day before. Once ignored the collateral damage done by journalists, the event brought a smile to the same heart that was shedding a tear for Ben and Maya's departure.

Next thing I remembered my first encounter with a baby-girl named Maya, born about a month before. Who knows? Perhaps she could become a famous dancer. Or at least she would learn to gracefully hold her head and ballet her way through school and further on, as far as her dreams could take her!

Without any warning, my heart started singing "The Time of my Life"[39]. It happens quite often that a song accompanies me throughout the day and it is usually connected to whatever I hear in the morning, either at home while I get ready for going out or on the way to work. Sometimes it is not something I hear, but a tune reminisced from the past that stays with me until another more appropriate one replaces it, according to whatever happens

---

[37] American Soul and R&B singer (1938–2015), most famous Top 10 hit 'Stand by me"

[38] Famous Russian ballet dancer (1925–2015), recognized as Prima Ballerina Assoluta at Bolshoi Theatre (starting 1960); she was also a choreographer, director and actor

[39] A 1987 song, from the soundtrack of the movie ‚Dirty Dancing', composed by Franke Previte, John DeNicola, and Donald Markowitz, and interpreted by Bill Medley and Jennifer Warnes

during that day... They all come with a certain mind-set and create the proper rhythm for whatever I need to do next.

Shortly after midday, I lit up the Sunday candle and went out for the daily stroll through the beautiful streets of Vienna. Soon I found myself wondering to some new places, never explored before. I looked up towards the quiet buildings, with their harmonious architecture and majestic lines; then I tried to imagine them full of life, as I suppose they should be on any given working day.

And then I suddenly realized that... I was dancing! Not obviously, not physically, not like Gene Kelly in the rain, but still... my heart was singing "The Time of my Life" again, while my soul was dancing, accompanying my feet down the sidewalk. Every step was somehow harmonized, getting "in-sync" with the tune. Probably because this is one of those songs that always make me get up and dance, no matter how tired, disappointed or hurt.

While dancing with the buildings, the trees and the clouds, I wondered how long it has been since I last wrote something. Back in 2013 I was quite close to finalizing the "Ways" series, and then, as of May 2015, I found myself in doubt it should end at all. Maybe it would be better to leave it eternally opened, and keep on adding thoughts in the years to come, preserve it as a work in progress throughout my life.

But then... the memory of the ballet dancer, the singer and the royal princess made me pause and listen more closely to my heart. And it revealed to me one of the simplest and at the same time most beautiful of all possible ways of facing the problems around.

It requires a bow and an invitation to dance—today, tomorrow and for the rest of our life! Give your spirit a proper tune and invite your material presence in this world to dance on it—and I bet it will take you to any place you can imagine! No matter whether your choice is ballet or tango, if you are on thin ice or on soft carpet, if you need to invoke rain or fertility, if it's time to mourn or to party, if you plan to start a game or launch an attack... It also doesn't matter if the song in your heart today is "Stand by Me" or "Beat It", "Kalinka" or "Zorba", "I'm a believer" or "Hit the road, Jack!"... Just sing along and move your body in harmony with how you feel, until you can see the beauty of life again.

Some may argue that dancing is a form of art and that they are not "gifted" for such an endeavor. Of course, we are not all Fred or Ginger, same as not every singer is Maria Callas, every scientist Einstein or Edison, every basketball player Michael Jordan or every gymnast Nadia. I am not talking of THAT kind of dancing. I am talking about finding your inner rhythm, which transcends art or religion, and goes along with any line of work or way of living which you would endeavor to pursue. A form of human expression which I suspect to be older than speech, and which resides in every living soul, no matter how it is being expressed outside.

Every act of creation has its own dance.

Every one carries a tempo within, and so we may dance to it every day—moving our heads or feet, rolling our eyes or tapping our fingers, feeling it deep inside our hearts or stomachs. Our music might come from something we hear, or feel, or dream, or sometimes even fear... our dance may express harmony or disruption, peace or torment, despair or hope. Movement may come out as elegant or erotic, majestic or common, provocative or inviting, intimidating or encouraging—there is no rule and there is no limit to what dancing can express!

And really, if you just cannot dance and are deaf to any kind of music—don't worry! You can define a different way of finding inner harmony, and unlocking your self-expression, which is closer to your heart. It could be sculpting or painting, running or swimming, flying or sailing, riding or hiking, gardening or knitting, cooking or gulf-playing and... you can further expand the list as you wish!

Humans invest a big share of waking hours into communicating with other living creatures, within the self-imposed boundaries to an otherwise potentially unlimited universe. In particular, highly educated people are quite difficult to convince that reason does not exist in the absence of feeling (which are easily hurt or misunderstood), or that theory and practice can coexist in parallel worlds (just like the Sun and the Moon!), that law does not always mean justice, same as education is not necessarily a good measure for character.

We need to do a lot of dancing with others that may respond to a different kind of music. Sometimes it is hard to follow their tune but, same as everything in life, practice brings one closer to perfection. Those who have exercised for years would know what I am talking about...

Once you start the day with a smile and involve some fine music in an inner conspiracy for successful living, your understanding of the world and perception about its challenges will depend more on yourself and your ability to deal with it than on others and their commitment to make things difficult.

And in order to reach that level of wisdom, there is one more thing you need to know about dancing: "Dancing is wonderful training for girls; it's the first way you learn to guess what a man is going to do before he does it."

Christopher Morley (Kitty Foyle character)

WAY 10—THE INHERITANCE

Motto:
"We are a continuum. Just as we reach back to our ancestors for our fundamental values, so we, as guardians of that legacy, must reach ahead to our children and their children.
And we do so with a sense of sacredness in that reaching."

Paul Tsongas

It is not easy to come to a conclusion when there are so many more things to say, however it is also time to roll this collection of uninvited advice to humanity, put it as a survival kit in a virtual bottle and throw it in the ocean of knowledge, to be appreciated or disregarded—only time will tell!

I will however leave an open door at the end of the tunnel, through which the readers can step ahead with courage, and continue their own inner exploration of roots and ways, in harmony with their life.

And on this door I will write: INHERITANCE.

Beyond the beautiful message already laid down in the motto, this concept is much larger than its noble "legacy" aspect.

I will start by defining the exact opposite, respectively the EGO-OUT concept invented by my dear friend Peter Glűck on the blog that hosted my book project. Ego-Out is the quantity of information, knowledge and wisdom lost in the death of an individual. It encompasses basically the spiritual part, which people either omit to (or purely cannot) pass on to other people before their death.

By exclusion, everything else (that is transmitted to the next generation) represents inheritance, and it has various components.

The most tangible and obvious to the naked eye, and also the most exposed to fierce fights amongst surviving relatives are material things—such as real estate, jewelry, cars, books, trousseaux, kitchen ware and so on.

The most resilient and (still!) difficult to manipulate are the genetic treats—such as physical appearance, intelligence, skills, health risks and similar.

The most sensitive to the environment are the spiritual ones—such as education and moral standards, traditions and beliefs, scientific and cultural wealth etc.

Last but not least, a category both sensitive to the environment and volatile from a public perception point of view is the social component of the inheritance—reputation, credibility, fame. This component is usually formed within a specific niche of activity or a specific social circle and it has very much to do with family bonds. It can be easily wasted by means of hasty or reckless behavior.

Except the genetic component, inheritance is not necessarily connected to a certain blood line or official family bonds. There are relationships in our lives that bring us close to other people that may bestow on us material, spiritual or social welfare, some following certain interest, and some out of pure generosity or kindness of their hearts. On the spiritual side especially, some do it intentionally, others just by being themselves. Some inheritance we accept, some we reject, consciously or not... Inheritance is also not necessarily good, as we may inherit expensive properties which we cannot afford to keep and cannot manage to sell or we can get stuck with weak genetics or pick up silly behavior and lousy habits all the time.

There is also another side of the coin, respectively the "taking back" story. It cannot be applied to all the inheritance components, as some are not within the control of "the giver" after being bestowed to the recipient. Materially or socially disinheriting an unfit or disobedient heir may bring some immediate effects in line with the deciding party's interests, but genetic and spiritual inheritance is certainly not reversible. I would dare to speculate that when the genetic and spiritual inheritance is strong and of good nature, the material effects of the disinheritance may be reversed in no time, while the motivational effects of challenged pride make the ambitious heir more prone to succeed in the long run.

Why should inheritance be regarded as the most important door to our future?

Let's look once again at the world around: the globalization has transformed most of the developing or under-developed countries into consumer hubs, pushing regular families beyond their real purchasing power, by encouraging excessive debt and waste, and by gradually turning this into a socially gratified behavior. Sometimes such vicious circle ends up with a negative legacy, transferring liability to the next generation; by accepting the material part one must take on also responsibility for related debt!

Therefore, it has become essential to understand the importance of sustainable wealth accumulation in such economies.

As I mentioned already in previous chapters, the prosperity of a nation is largely dependent on the profile of its middle class. This may grow stronger only by accumulating material wealth across several generations, gradually passing it on as inheritance to the next line of legitimate heirs. A healthy mix of expenditure with long-term saving is one of the most important engines for progress on a macroeconomic level. In this context, increased awareness about the importance of ensuring material stability for the children is a way of fostering financial responsibility within middle-class families.

Moving on to the next components of the inheritance, spiritual and social parts are highly sensitive to both their material factor (as education, culture and exposure to global environment are rather expensive treats!), and social environment (starting with family, school, work and social circle). For those components, negative legacy is hard to counter, as rotten morale and bad reputation takes a lot of continuous effort and sometimes more than one generation to redeem.

Without a constant focus on what we expose ourselves and our children to, we will gradually lose control over what we shall leave as inheritance to those who follow... and the world as we know it is being tested nowadays, on an unprecedented level, at least for the last century. We are witnessing a material, cultural and social clash of civilizations, with one major stake: the preservation of national inheritance!

And, same as with all important things in life, it is hard to define and then maintain just the right balance. Pride is the most resilient genetic treat of mankind and it governs on all other heritage matters. Humans have a primary need to be proud of their offspring and the legacy they leave behind.

As people cannot compromise either on individual and family inheritance, or on the national legacy, communities should learn to wisely listen and strive to harmonize an entire chorus of contradicting voices (pride and prejudice, material interests and needs, survival and tolerance boundaries, generosity and humanitarian spirit), while not forgetting to re-visit the lessons of history!

While we pretend to be our ancestors' most honorable and ambitious dreams turned to reality, we also have a duty to prevent our children from becoming our worst nightmares!

HAND-DREAMING

I lay quietly asleep

With mind silenced, breathing deep;

There's no face or sound or color

Just Your Hand holding my sorrow.

We don't speak as there's no need

To feel words beneath our feet;

It is dark outside and cold

Your Hand warm holding my soul.

In my dream there is no face

And no tear, nothing to trace;

Your Hand gentle on my skin

And no fears in between.

I did not invite you in

Still, you're here in my dream

Knowing that I want you near

As the forest needs the deer.

I wake up. Apparently

There's nobody next to me;

But I know I'm not alone

As Your Hand is never gone!

The dream faints away too fast

Still, one thing will always last:

As I ride my own life's wave

You, My Lord, will keep me safe!